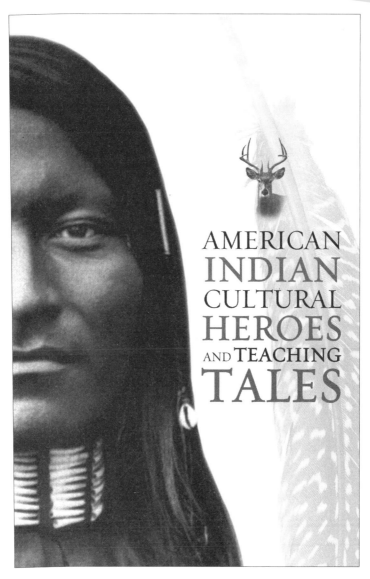

AMERICAN INDIAN CULTURAL HEROES AND TEACHING TALES

Also by Kurt Kaltreider

American Indian Prophecies

Hay House Titles of Related Interest

Books

Archangels & Ascended Masters, by Doreen Virtue, Ph.D.

The Journey to the Sacred Garden (book-and-CD),
by Hank Wesselman, Ph.D.

The Love and Power Journal, by Lynn Andrews

Sacred Ceremony, by Steven D. Farmer, Ph.D.

The Saint, the Surfer, and the CEO, by Robin Sharma

Soul Coaching, by Denise Linn

Visionseeker, by Hank Wesselman, Ph.D.

Wokini, by Billy Mills, with Nicholas Sparks

Card Decks

The Four Agreements, by DON Miguel Ruiz

Inner Peace Cards, by Dr. Wayne W. Dyer

Kryon Cards, by Lee Carroll

Wisdom Cards, by Louise L. Hay

All of the above are available at your local bookstore,
or may be ordered by visiting:
Hay House USA: **www.hayhouse.com**
Hay House Australia: **www.hayhouse.com.au**
Hay House UK: **www.hayhouse.co.uk**
Hay House South Africa: **orders@psdprom.co.za**

AMERICAN INDIAN CULTURAL HEROES AND TEACHING TALES

Evenings with Chasing Deer

Kurt Kaltreider, Ph.D.

HAY HOUSE, INC.
Carlsbad, California
London • Sydney • Johannesburg
Vancouver • Hong Kong

Published and distributed in the United States by: Hay House, Inc., P.O. Box 5100, Carlsbad, CA 92018-5100 • *Phone:* (760) 431-7695 or (800) 654-5126 • *Fax:* (760) 431-6948 or (800) 650-5115 • www.hayhouse.com • **Published and distributed in Australia by:** Hay House Australia, Ltd., 18/36 Ralph St., Alexandria NSW 2015 • *Phone:* 612-9669-4299 • *Fax:* 612-9669-4144 • www.hayhouse.com.au • **Published and distributed in the United Kingdom by:** Hay House UK, Ltd. • Unit 62, Canalot Studios • 222 Kensal Rd., London W10 5BN • *Phone:* 44-20-8962-1230 • *Fax:* 44-20-8962-1239 • www.hayhouse.co.uk • **Published and distributed in the Republic of South Africa by:** Hay House SA (Pty), Ltd., P.O. Box 990, Witkoppen 2068 • *Phone/Fax:* 2711-7012233 • orders@psdprom.co.za • **Distributed in Canada by:** Raincoast • 9050 Shaughnessy St., Vancouver, B.C. V6P 6E5 • *Phone:* (604) 323-7100 • *Fax:* (604) 323-2600

Design: Amy Rose Szalkiewicz

Library of Congress Cataloging-in-Publication Data

Kaltreider, Kurt.
  American Indian cultural heroes and teaching tales : evenings with Chasing Deer / Kurt Kaltreider.
    p. cm.
  ISBN 1-4019-0213-8
  1. Indians of North America—Folklore. 2. Indians of North America—Social life and customs. 3. Indians of North America—Study and teaching. 4. Folklore—Study and teaching—North America. 5. Iktomi (Legendary character)—Legends. I. Title.
  E98.F6K35 2004
  398.2'089'97—dc22
                                        2003019791

                          ISBN 1-4019-0213-8

                        07 06 05 04   4 3 2 1
                          1st printing, March 2004

                          Printed in Canada

This book is dedicated to:

Three incredible people: my children
Peter, Christian, and Sallie.

And, to their mother, Sallie Middleton Parker,
for doing such a wonderful job of raising them.
Thank you.

To my former wife, Joan Borysenko, without whose help
and influence I would never have taken up writing.

To Jill, for bringing me so much happiness in the Twilight.

Last, to my Medicine Man, Sonny Richards; his assistant,
Jason James; and the Miller Brothers—Jake, John, Tate,
and Mio—our Hochoka singers and drummers.

Pilamaya, Mitakuye Oyasin.

Contents

"So if today I had a young mind to direct, to start the journey of life, and I was faced with the duty of choosing between the natural way of my forefathers and that of the white man's civilization, I would, for its welfare, unhesitatingly set that child's feet in the path of my forefathers. I would raise him to be an Indian!"

— Chief Luther Standing Bear, Lakota

"Our ideas will overcome your ideas.
We are going to cut the country's whole value system to shreds.
It isn't important that there are only 500,000 of us Indians. . . .
What is important is that we have a superior way of life.
We Indians have a more humane philosophy of life.
We Indians will show this country how to act human.
Someday this country will revise its Constitution, its laws,
in terms of human beings, instead of property. If Red Power
is to be a power in this country it is because it is ideological. . . .
What is the ultimate value of a man's life?
That is the question."

— Vine Deloria, Lakota

Foreword

While some would say that a culture lives by its stories, I'd take it a step further and say that a culture *is* its stories. Our cultural stories become the foundation upon which we develop our national identity and our religious/tribal identity. They inform our family stories, and they're the basis for our personal stories. To understand the eternal question of "Who am I?" we must first place the "I" in the larger frame of the world within which "I" exists: our stories.

Thus, even our personal identity and sense of self—in all but the most transcendental contexts—is a function of, derived from, and ultimately subservient to, our larger cultural stories.

And where do these stories come from?

Well, a few years ago I was sitting around a council fire at a New Age sort of meeting of shamans and elders from Native American, African, Peruvian, Brazilian, and Wiccan cultures. I was the group's representative of what the Native

American elders called "white people." There were a half dozen or so of us "elders" from various traditions sitting around this circle, and around us was a larger circle of several hundred mostly young people, almost all of whom were "whites," yet dressed as if they were Native Americans.

One of the native elders, a man named Frank, leaned over to me and whispered a question to the effect of, "Why do so many of your people feel the need to dress up like us?"

I pointed out that his people—at least some of them—still remember the ways of their most ancient ancestors. They know the names of the holy places, the properties of the medicinal herbs, and the posture of the spirits of the world. They know their roots, and many even know their ancient languages. However, my people (descended in my case from Wales and Norway) have completely lost this knowledge.

Our European tribal ancestors were first conquered 3,000 years ago by the Celts, then again by the Romans 1,000 years later, and finally by the Christians during the past 1,200 or so years. The Celts at least allowed us to keep our languages and religions, but the Romans worked hard to stamp these out, leaving the "romance" languages as their legacy. And the Christians engaged in a thousand-year-long orgy of murdering our wise-women herbalists and midwives ("witches"), imposing sterile male domination through a male-only clergy, and enthusiastically seeking out and destroying all but the most obscure of our tribal holy sites, runes, and artifacts.

A people who have been so completely and totally detribalized are a lost people. We've lost access to our ancient stories, our ancient wisdom, and our ancient connection to Mother Earth and All Life. We've lost our egalitarian tribal traditions—so well documented by Thomas Jefferson in citing the 1724 "History of England" by Paul de Rapin de Thoyras—and traded them in for a bizarre collection of domination stories including an angry, twisted god and a perversion of Darwin's theories to justify bleeding the poor to enrich the wealthy.

We can't remember our stories—they've been taken from us—and, thus, we've lost our roots. Because there are no time machines, we whites won't easily or quickly recover our stories. They're gone, and will never be heard again. But it *is* possible for us to inform and transform our current dysfunctional stories, which is the powerful and vital role of the book you're holding in your hands.

Kurt Kaltreider straddles both worlds, as he had a white parent and a Native American parent. He knows the traditions and ways of both his white culture and his Indian culture. He's dedicated his life to collecting, organizing, cataloging, preserving, and sharing the ancient stories of his Native American ancestors.

Consequently, we now have this critical resource, in which you'll find some of the most important and vital core stories that have informed and united several of the Native American nations over the millennia. They're fun, fascinating, transformational reads. But more important, the lessons—what some today call "memes"—of these stories are contagious. They can infect us *and* infect our culture. They offer the hope of transforming into a better way of living and a better world.

Thus, in a very real way, you may be holding in your hands a part of the eventual salvation of the world. When we "white folks" (and all the others of various colors and shades who share our worldview) begin to realize that it's possible for humans to live together in peace, for justice to prevail, and for fairness to be a core cultural value, the world will begin to change.

That change begins this moment with you. Read on!

— **Thom Hartmann,** Montpelier, Vermont

Introduction

If I were a mythologist or folklorist, I would more than likely have written a far different Introduction than I have. When I read a book I like to know something about the person who's writing it—in short, who they are and where they're "coming from." So I'm going to tell you some things about myself, about why I've written this book, and about the book itself. Last, I'm going to give you some idea of the kind of cultures, societies, and people that the cultural heroes, whose stories I relate, have been so instrumental in creating. Otherwise, to me at least, they have little meaning.

The president of Hay House, Reid Tracy, wrote me and asked if I'd like to write a book about Native American tales and legends in what he hoped would be the second in a series of books about Native America by me. He explained there was soon going to be a television special on Lakota tales and legends, and that it would be nice to have a book on that subject come out about the same time. (I knew about the special since my medicine man, Sonny Richards, was the consultant for the show.) At the time, I was working on two other books that I was passionate about. So, part of me wanted to write the book simply because Reid asked me to; after all, it was he who had given me the opportunity to write my first book, *American Indian Prophecies*. Yet another part of me wanted to continue what I was working on.

I have only one motivation to write anything. It's really a series of things, but they all hang together for me. I'm only motivated to write in order to preserve the traditions, the wisdom, and the way of life of the indigenous peoples of the Americas. (I'm equally sympathetic to the other indigenous peoples of the world, but the Americas are enough for one lifetime, and they are my People.) Coupled with this motivation is my desire to show others that modern Western civilization is a seriously backward and destructive society from a spiritual, social, political, and moral point of view. I'm truly afraid that time is running out for us. Many indigenous cultures in the Americas reached levels of development that make our present society look, quite frankly, retarded. For example, I can't think of one of our Presidents who wouldn't have either been banned from the tribe or killed if they had behaved in Lakota society (200 or more years ago) the way they do now, for lying was about the only capital offense. If you want to see how human beings should live, then look to the American Indians (not all tribes, of course, but many of them).

Interestingly enough, the Amish people represent the only intact tribe in the United States today. Now, if we examine them, what do and don't we find? We find a people who are far healthier than the average American and who live far longer as a result. We find a people who have never engaged in war. We find an integrity that few, if any, of the other segments of this country's population can match. We find an energy among the Amish that seems inexhaustible, and most important, we note a sense of humor, contrary to the general perception of outsiders. What we don't find are the homeless, the hungry, and the disenfranchised. And all of this has been accomplished without the aid of modern technology.

I lived beside the Amish for about 20 summers, and believe me, they are a happy people. I can't say for sure, but I seriously doubt if they're as plagued by depression, anxiety, neurosis, and psychosis as are a high percentage of Americans. And it's a little-known fact that every adult Amish person is Amish by choice, for they're not truly part of the "tribe" until they decide to be, which usually occurs around the age of 16. Unfortunately, the Amish, too, are constantly under pressure to assimilate into the larger, dominant culture by being forced to go to school. So much for freedom in the "Land of the Free."

Living in—and Learning from—the Past

The founder of the Boy Scouts of America, Ernest Thompson Seton, was driven by a vision for the American people. He wanted to find a way to help develop the very best human beings possible for his country. Born in 1860, Seton was an early critic of the materialism and the social ills that plagued the United States, diligently sifting through history to find the most perfect of men to act as his model. If his writing seems overly "male," please remember when it was written. I can assure you that Seton was no sexist and that "womanhood" could have as easily been used as the word "manhood." This was his conclusion:

> And still I held my vision of the perfect man—athletic, fearless, kind, picturesque, wise in the ways of the woods, and without reproach of life. And by a long, long trail, with ample knowledge of histories and of persons, I was led, as many before me have been, to choose the ideal Redman. By all the evidence at hand, his was a better system, a better thought, because it produced far nobler, better men. He, more than any type I know, is the stuff that fires our highest dreams of manhood, realized complete.

Seton further says all that needs to be said about Western civilization as compared to the typical Indian culture when he writes in the epilogue of his *The Gospel of the Redman,* written in 1927:

> The Civilization of the Whiteman is a failure; it is visibly crumbling around us. It has failed every crucial test. No one who measures things by results can question this fundamental statement. . . . How are we going to appraise the value of a Civilization? By certain yard measures that are

founded on human nature, and which remorselessly investigate the fundamentals of the man-mind and the man-needs.

First of these is: Does your Civilization guarantee to you the absolute freedom of action so long as you do not encroach on the equal right of your neighbor to do the same thing? Does your system work for the greatest happiness of the greatest number? Is your Civilization characterized by justice in the courts and gentleness in the streets? Are its largest efforts to relieve suffering and misery?

Does your Civilization grant to every individual the force and rights of humanhood? Is everyone in your community guaranteed food, shelter, protection, dignity, so long as your group has these things in its gifts? Does your system guarantee the tribal control of tribal interests? Does your system guarantee to each man one vote; but so much influence as his character can command? Does your system guarantee to each man the product of his industry? Does your system accept the fact that material things are of doubtful or transient value, that the things of the spirit are all that are enduring and worthwhile? Does your system set larger value on kindness than on rigorous justice?

Does your system discourage large material possessions in one man? Does your system provide for the sick, the helpless, the weak, the old, and the stranger? Does your system guarantee the integrity of the natural group called the family? Does your system recognize and further the fundamental thought that the chief duty of man is the attainment of manhood, which means the perfect and harmonious development of every part and power that

goes to make a man; and the consecration of that manhood
to the service of one's people?

By every one of these tests, the white civilization is a
failure. There are three things in the above that weren't
aspects of tribal life but were of European and American
life: (1) The American Indian did not have courts. Dis-
putes were usually solved between the parties involved and
at times with the counsel of the elders. Some matters were
dealt with by the general consensus of the tribe if the problem in question involved the welfare of the tribe as a
whole. (2) The American Indian had no concept of voting
as we have today; rather, there was the concept of "one
mind." As the primary concern of any individual tribal
member was the welfare of the tribe as a whole, agreement was generally not that difficult to reach, since the
People would be of "one mind." If it so happened that all
could not agree, then the matter was simply tabled, so to
speak, as obviously more time was needed for proper
consideration. With the encroachment of the white man,
this tended to break down, as immediate action was
required for tribal survival. (3) Most of the products of one's
industry were for the overall welfare of the people, not for
the individual. Hoarding and accumulation were not part
of tribal life.

Nonetheless, I realize that I still haven't answered the
question, "Why did you write this book?"

Several years ago at a conference, a colleague asked me,
"Why don't you get back into formal axiology [mathematical

value theory], psychology, and philosophy, where you can make a contribution to the real world? This is the 20th century, not the 15th! All your time and energy is spent trying to live a way of life that has been dead for some time. The time of the Indian is gone—you can't turn back the clock, so why make yourself miserable wishing and working for a past that will never return?"

The person went on like this for a few more minutes, but I didn't get angry. I knew what he was saying; in fact, I'd heard it before. My former wife, Joan Borysenko, had told me more than once to quit living in the past.

At any rate, I answered my curious friend like this: "Philip, for years I studied philosophy and psychology. I concentrated on ethics and formal axiology, and I loved it. One day while sitting in a professional meeting listening to a paper on the ethics of Kierkegaard, something I'd been pondering for several years struck me so forcefully that I had to leave the meeting and be by myself to think. This is what I thought: *Western culture has been a complete failure ethically, spiritually, socially, and politically. Its history has been one of constant warfare with ever-increasing magnitude, racism, sexism, exploitation, genocide, environmental destruction, and, despite the propaganda, an increasing loss of freedom. So here I've been sitting listening to yet another paper on ethics. The truth is that if Western civilization had followed any of the great ethical thinkers, from Plato to Rawls—it hardly matters who—we would have had a far better world. Even the great spiritual teachers like Jesus haven't been listened to, much less followed. So, what am I to do, sit around and play my intellectual fiddle while Rome burns?* I knew that with formal axiology, we had the tools to make proper and decent decisions in our governments and in our culture as a whole; indeed, in about any place we applied it. What were the chances of that actually happening? There were two: slim and none.

"I asked myself, 'What would Jesus do? What would my Crazy Horse do?' I knew what they would do. I'm not a Christian, so I would follow Crazy Horse. I would be a warrior for my people, for their wisdom, for their culture, for their very lives.

"Philip, I'm not blind. I know that my People are dying quickly. I know that on some reservations our life expectancy has dropped by 40 years from two or three hundred years ago. I know that hundreds of languages have vanished like the dew in the morning sunlight, never to be spoken again on this planet. I know that the United States government wants us gone as soon as possible. I know that they still cheat us and trick us. I know that in the '70s they sterilized about 25 percent of our women in violation of the United Nations' Genocide Conventions, which they refused to sign like the rest of the 'civilized' world. I know that those responsible will never be brought before an international tribunal like the Nazis or others in more recent years. I know that my People are both prisoners of war and political prisoners in their own land. I know that, like Henry Kissinger and [the late] Senator Daniel Patrick Moynihan, the American power elite can write in their autobiographies and memoirs of the roles they've played in genocide and think they are untouchable.

[In Moynihan's and Kissinger's case, it was the genocide that began in 1975 in East Timor. Few Americans even know that it happened, much less that it far surpassed the Jewish Holocaust in terms of the percentage of the total population that was destroyed.] I know these things and so much more.

"But I know this, too—that even though my skin color is heavily influenced by my fair German father, and that I'm obviously not a full-blood, my heart beats pure red. Even as a young child, I told people that I was an Indian. The first time I changed an official document was when I was six years old. Under 'race' on some school form, they had written 'W.' I scratched it out and wrote 'I.'

"I can remember the first time I attended an Indian health conference on the Diné [Navajo] reservation. We did a dance in which there were two circles going in opposite directions, one inside the other. As you circled you came face-to-face with the person circling in the opposite direction. When those first ancient Diné eyes met mine, I started to cry. I was looking into the soul of *my* People. Indians aren't ashamed to cry, so I did. I was home and I knew it. The same thing had happened years earlier in my first sweat lodge. When I hear songs in Lakota, my adopted tribe, I feel something so ancient, so real, so much a part of the planet that I'm overwhelmed. I can only say that it is ecstatic. The happiest places on Earth for me are the sweat lodge and the *Yuwipi,* a healing ceremony.

"I can say without hesitation that I would gladly give my life that my People might live. So, you see, my friend, I have no choice. This is who I am, and I wouldn't have it any other way. It's far more important to me to make tobacco prayer ties for my ailing medicine man than to receive academic accolades, $10 million, or a Nobel Prize."

I could have also told my friend that there's a short Lakota prayer that's often said at the beginning of many of our ceremonies (such as the *Hanblecheyapi,* or "vision quest" as it is often called today). It goes *"Tunkashila, onshimala ye oyate wani wachin cha,"* and it translates to "Grandfather, have pity on me that my People may live." That is why I live as I do and also why I write: that my people may live.

Straddling Two Very Different Worlds

After more than 25 years of education and more than twice that time of living, I have been able to conclude only one thing about humankind: We are tribal animals. All of our ancestors, no matter what their race or where they lived, were tribal. Furthermore, I believe that this was no accident. It wasn't a thought-out choice—as I see it, human beings are biologically, psychologically, and sociologically tribal. It's when human beings begin to live outside of the tribal mode of existence that they begin to deteriorate.

All the evils that I cited earlier were brought about, and still exist, as a result of the actions of nontribal people upon tribal people. The "civilized" have always felt that they must enlighten the "savages" . . . unfortunately, no one's ever asked whether they wish to be civilized or enlightened.

So I write to do my small part in keeping tribal people alive.

Not long after Reid's suggestion, I was doing a mini-vision quest, starting my prayers with the short one I mentioned on the last page: *"Tunkashila, onshimala ye oyate wani wachin cha."* That simple beginning prayer made my decision for me. Precious few people in North America know anything of the great men and women who fashioned our native cultures and our spiritual practices—after all, for tens of thousands of years my People walked upon Turtle Island before it was even known about by Westerners. So I decided that I would write about our cultural heroes.

I suspected that very few people know the tales that the Lakota used to teach their children and reinforce their ways in the older Lakota population. Furthermore, even if a white person *had* read these "teaching tales," I doubted that they really understood them as a Lakota would. I concluded that this was just as important a way to help my People live, as was critical appraisal of the failure of Western culture from an Indian perspective, my primary interest. Furthermore, writing these tales would be a challenge, as I don't consider myself a fiction writer (far from it, in fact).

In my previous book, I recorded the conversations between Chasing Deer, a Cheyenne/Lakota elder; and John Lawson, the progeny of a blue-blooded New England father and a mother from the landed gentry of Virginia, who had just graduated from Dartmouth. Their conversations ranged from the American Indian Holocaust to a comparison of Indian life and values with those of the dominant

Euro-American culture. Interwoven amid the various top-ics were relevant prophecies. Now, anyone familiar with Indian life knows that a night around the campfire is a time for stories. So I thought that if I were to make John's stay with Chasing Deer complete, then I had to tell the stories he'd heard as well.

Before I talk about the book itself, I'd like to say some-thing about the two characters in both this book and the previous one. Chasing Deer is a composite of two people—my grandfather, and a 118-year-old Anishnabe that I spent a week with in 1997. I couldn't even begin to spell the old man's name, as it was rather long and in Anishnabe. He spoke no English, so all of our conversations were done via a translator. He lived far north of Ottawa, Canada, deep in the bush, about as far away from "civilization" as he could. He wasn't at all frail, as most elderly people tended to be; instead, he was probably around 180 pounds and stood about 5'11". I could detect few of the infirmities that usually come with age, and his mind was sharp. He was angry at what had happened to his People since the "white invaders" came, as he called the Euro-Americans. In the old days, he said that his tribe had no murders, no theft, no abuse and, of course, no alcohol or drug problems.

During his lifetime, this man had fought to free his people from the domination of the Canadian government and return them to the old ways. He didn't hate Euro-Americans, but he did hate their culture. He actually felt a deep compassion for them, for he didn't see how a people who lived so far from the way the Earth and the Creator wished them to live could be happy. "I wouldn't be surprised if one day they have to take workshops to learn how to make babies," he said, in making the point that white people are so far removed from their humanness and the sacred.

Like most Indians, he had a great sense of humor. One evening, still with his sunglasses on, he ranted on and on about the evils of Western civilization. Then he paused and said, "I must be honest, Grandson—there is one good thing about this culture. Sunglasses!"

Pop, my grandfather, was a half-breed. I know that he never went to college, and I'm not sure if he even went to high school. He was a self-educated man well versed in history and literature who possessed something that can't be taught in a classroom: wisdom. He was sharp, and like most older Indians could spot a contradiction a mile away. I spent many Sundays with him alone, either at his house or at the zoo. He loved the zoo——he'd pick me up and say, "Let's go visit our friends! How lonely and sad they must be all locked up with people gawking at them. They should take that zoo director and put *him* in a cage for a month, and then maybe he would free them."

At the zoo, Pop would try to teach me things. For example, in the bird house he'd have me concentrate on the song of a particular bird until that was all I could hear amid the hundreds that were singing. Then we'd move on to another bird. I didn't know it then, but I was being taught three things: silence within myself, concentration, and the ability to finely discriminate the environment before me.

Pop taught me trust and fearlessness by holding me up over the bars of the hippopotamus's cage, about a foot in front of his open mouth. He'd also hold me over the large and deep pool where the polar bears lived. I never told my mother this—and I'm sure that to most people of the dominant culture, this was highly irresponsible on his part. This wasn't how he saw it. For Pop, a life lived without trust or in fear was no life at all. The dominant culture values physical life more than anything else: Old people are kept alive when nature would have taken them long ago, 90 percent of all doctor visits are unnecessary, most yearly physicals are a waste of time and money, and so forth. The Indian is concerned with the inner quality of her or his life, with its integrity and its meaning. The length of one's life isn't the issue; harmony with one's self, with one's relatives, with the Sacred, and with the environment is.

Although Pop was raised to be a white man amid the rampant racism of the eastern shore of Maryland, he somehow maintained a basically native outlook on life. He taught me to never trust the State, any State, for their authority was illegitimate. He taught me the corrupt history of organized religion. And finally, he taught me about the evils of corporations and capitalism. True to his beliefs, I found out while doing some research for my tribal registration that Pop had never even bothered to get a Social Security card.

My father was a professor at both the University of Maryland Medical School and Johns Hopkins Medical School. He was an intellectual with very broad interests—in fact, his time at home was seldom spent studying medicine but rather reading literature, philosophy, and books on art and civilization. He was a man of unshakable principles when it came to right and wrong. He was anything but dogmatic, yet he had a clear perception of good and evil, and I'm not talking about petty things. He didn't get his sense of right and wrong from any religion, but from an overriding dedication to the truth and a desire to harm no one. He was a freethinker in the style and manner of Bertrand Russell. As a child, I was only taught two things about right and wrong: Never intentionally harm another person, and never seek to harm or destroy another person's meaning. That was it. I can honestly say that I've met few people in my life with Dad's integrity and honesty. My mother once told me that she thought he was constitutionally incapable of telling a lie.

Contrary to what one might expect, Pop and Dad had a great love and respect for each other. When I was young, I'd sit enthralled by their conversation and the dialectic that it naturally involved. So it was that I grew up very much immersed in the intellectual and scientific world of Western civilization—and, at the same time, with the simple, spiritual, poetic native outlook of my grandfather. And I became very much a product of these two radically different worlds.

John and Chasing Deer: The Beginning

I think that it would be good if I told you some of the history of the relationship between Chasing Deer and John Lawson.

After graduating from Dartmouth in June 1997, John and his college roommate, Tommy Chasing Deer, went to visit Tommy's great-great-grandfather, Chasing Deer. It was an arduous journey there, as the last 14 miles were on horseback through rugged terrain with few clearly marked paths. When they finally arrived, John was surprised to see how spry, alive, and clear an 118-year-old man could be. Chasing Deer was born in 1879, not far from Bear Butte, South Dakota, and his mother was Cheyenne (or Tsistsistas) and his father was Lakota. At the time, John had thought, *Man, that's just three years after The Battle of Little Big Horn—or The Battle of Greasy Grass as it's known to the Indians—where that epic servant of genocide, George Armstrong Custer, met his death.*

John continued to visit Chasing Deer every summer, and in the summer of 2000, Chasing Deer adopted John during the same Making of Relatives ceremony in which John and Tommy were made *Hunkas,* the closest relationship that one can form with another in Lakota society.

In college, John encountered many fine and brilliant professors whose minds he greatly admired, but none of them could compare to the ancient, formally uneducated Chasing Deer when it came to wisdom. As John saw it, Chasing Deer had more wisdom than Solomon, Socrates, and Jesus combined when it came to human beings and how they needed to live. More important—and what John felt separated him from the others—was Chasing Deer's thorough understanding of those social, political, and spiritual aspects of a human culture, which make for harmony and self-fulfillment. He was able to combine an overriding concern for the welfare of the group and an extreme individualism, so unlike the rugged individualism of the America that John knew. Chasing Deer showed John how his ancestors were able to live like this without conflict, something never to be found in the entire history of Western culture.

To say that Chasing Deer turned John's world upside down would be an understatement, yet the old man was never arrogant or judgmental. His sparkling eyes radiated gentleness and an extreme kindness, and John felt as though he were the most important person in the world when Chasing Deer was talking to him. In true Indian fashion, he never interrupted; and when John was through talking, he was always slow to answer. John knew that this elder was taking what he had to say under full consideration. And when he thought that John was mistaken, he was gentle and never made the young man feel either stupid or silly. Chasing Deer was truly one of those people for whom there were no stupid questions—only honest or dishonest ones.

My first book consisted of the conversations between Chasing Deer and John, which centered around the differences between native culture and Euro-American culture, with relevant Indian prophecies from many tribes woven into the conversations. What's most interesting about American Indian prophecies is that they're very straightforward and require no interpretation, unlike, say, the Bible or Nostradamus.

One time John asked Chasing Deer what he thought was the greatest difference between his culture and that of the Euro-Americans. The following was Chasing Deer's answer:

> Grandson, there are so many differences that it would be hard to say what is *the difference*. Let me give you a few things to ponder and then we can talk about them tomorrow.
>
> I suppose that the first thing that I would say is that we live in the sacred; your people study it. Your history is written in your books; ours is written in our hearts. You need laws by which to live; we did not. You have criminals; we did not. Your leaders lie to your people; for ours, it would have been unthinkable. Our children were raised to become themselves, to become distinct individuals; yours are raised to be the same. Silence was one of our greatest virtues; yours, incessant noise. Our children from birth were taught generosity; yours, accumulation and greed. You greatly value success; we value respect and honor. Your people do things for profit; our people to be helpful.
>
> When you think of these things over the next day or so, put them in the following perspective: We had no jails, we had no locks, we seldom ever had a murder. There may have been some, but I have never heard of a rape. Our gays were fully accepted. Our women had power.

Sometime in the spring or early summer of 2001, Chasing Deer died at the age of 121. (That may seem awfully old to us, but keep in mind that as many as 20 percent of American Indians lived to be well over 90 before being exposed to the Euro-American world.) Tommy and John went to visit him in late June 2001, yet they couldn't find him anywhere. Hoping that they wouldn't find him there, they went to the burial platform that Chasing Deer had erected for himself many years before . . . and there he was. His pipe was still held in his ancient hands, and his eyes were closed, with a look of extreme peace upon his deteriorating face. Chasing Deer had died as he wanted to die, as an Indian.

His grandchildren left him there to finish his thanksgiving and his return to his Mother. John was so happy to see that his very dear friend had been able to live out his life according to his beliefs: no casket, no hospital, no strangers surrounding him, and no autopsy. Chasing Deer lived and died as he was—a child of Grandmother Earth, Grandfather Sun, and the Spirits. I can imagine his last words, as he peered up to the heavens: *"Pilamaya, mitakuye oyasin"* or "Thank you, all my relations."

An Indian Manifesto

To conclude this brief description of the difference between Euro-American culture and that of my Indian ancestors, I'd like to share a small portion of an overly lengthy poem that poured out of my soul the night before an honoring ceremony was to be done for me. The war with Iraq was drawing closer every day, and I was in communication with a particular chief about taking a stance against the war and dissuading any of his tribe, including those in the armed forces, from in any way participating in what President Bush was determined to do. It made me reflect about what it was to be an Indian living in a white man's world. I never rewrote or edited what came forth from my heart that night, which follows:

An Indian Manifesto

I am not a politically correct baby killer.
I did not spring, like you, from the State,
The most destructive creation of Western
So-called civilization.
You, like It, for an It it is,
Are lost in Death and Greed
Because you believe in It more
Than your own flesh and bone.

No, I sprang from the Fire and Stone of
My Mother, Ena Maka, Unci Wakan,
Ena Wakan, the Sacred Earth!
I am as strong as Her Stones
And as passionate as Her Fire.
I am a man of Blood and Bone
Going back eons in my Mother's Womb
That forged my body and my soul.
My sacred Mother who feeds me.
Who clothes me.
Who shows me such Beauty
That not a day goes by that I do not cry
At some unexpected miracle.

Introduction

Who like all Mothers gives and gives,
Asking only that her child prosper.
My Mother's Breast has never been denied me.
The respect that I have for her,
The gratitude in my Heart
I cannot express, except to let a tear
Fall upon her Breast in thanksgiving.
She knows that.

I love my Mother.
Whoever defiles Her
Defiles all Women.
And now, the products of decadence and abuse,
Women defile themselves and the Earth.
And so the cycle of male abuse rolls on.
Where are your Lysistratas?
We need them far more than in the
Day of spear and sword,
Or do you not mind "making love"
With baby killers?

Mother, my beautiful, loving Mother
Who allows trees to talk to me
And animals to make and keep
Agreements with me.
They are not dumb.
They speak only to open hearts.
Only man is dumb, and numb and stupid.
Oh, my Mother who shows me more Beauty
Than my heart can sometimes stand.

I am here for you, Mother, always,
Until I return to You.
I will return when all the passion
In me is sucked dry and my heart
Shall be as a prune,
Dried up as I have given the Crimson
Blood of my ancestors to my love,
To my children, to my brothers and sisters,
And to you, my Mother.
For to die not sucked dry is a crime
Against humanity and worse still
Against yourself.

So, Mother, I pick up the tools
You gave me:
Sight, hearing, taste, smell, touch,
Intellect, and Spirit, and I depart
Again to have every last cell of
My blood used to fuel my Passion
And to be drained in Flesh Offerings
For my People.
And when I need refueling I'll lay upon
Your Breast, whose milk turns to Blood
In my veins.
This I shall do until I am withered with
Age and my Heart is becoming a prune,
But for every single drop of blood my heart loses
In good and noble cause, my soul grows
Until, at last, Mother, my body has

Introduction

Turned to Spirit.
Then I shall return to you.

There shall be no casket for this Redman.
I am not a Wasi'chu who so disdains
The rest of Creation that he refuses
To give his bones that the next generation
Might live.
The Wasi'chu locks them up in a steel box,
Just like his money.
He lived in fear, and he died in fear.
And now he is spending Eternity
Smelling the stench of his own heart
In his $10,000.00 metal prison.

Mother, I am sending you a voice!
Hear me!
I am your Grandson, Naicinji,[1]
The Defender, the Protector of
Women and Children, Vision ordained.
When I rejoin you and become
Ten billion atoms and molecules,
Which you shall use through your Alchemy,
To bring forth new Life,
I only ask of You, my dearest Mother,
Before my decaying body with Joy

---

[1] My name and role given to me in a vision quest.

Returns to you so that the seventh
Generation may live,
Please whisper in my ear, if truth it be:
I am proud of you, Naicinji,
You have served the Women
And Children with love.
My Naicinji, my precious Son,
It is now time to give the wonderful
Body I gave you back to me
That others may live.
I know that you do with joy
In your Heart.
I commend your Sacred Spirit to Tunkashila.
Go and rest now, my precious little boy
Who became a Man I so loved
And so loved me.
Go, Naicinji,
Go to the Pleiades
And be with your beloved Crazy Horse,
Red Armed Panther, and Touch the Clouds.
I love you, I love you
My dearest Naicinji.
But, for now, join me and we shall be
As One, once again, under the Hemlock.

Introduction

Joseph Campbell once said that the American Indians were the most spiritual people on Earth. In the cultural-hero stories that follow, you'll learn of three people who were very influential in producing the most spiritual, just, happy, and fearless people that the world has ever known. These were the ancestors of both Chasing Deer and myself.

In the teaching tales, I have related some of the stories that reminded the Lakota people how *not* to live if they were to be Lakota. I hope that you enjoy them.

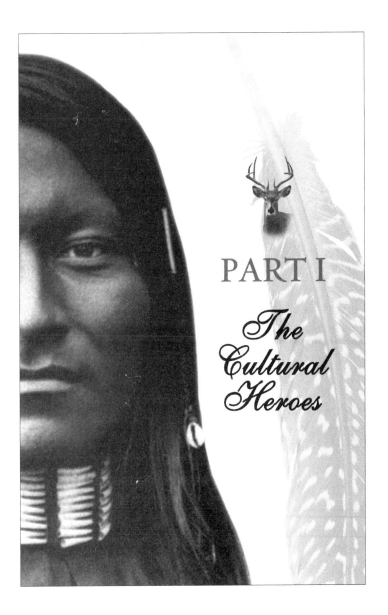

PART I

The
Cultural
Heroes

CHAPTER ONE

Dekanahwideh

It was one of those brilliantly clear nights that are now only available to us far away from the lights of cities and industry. It would have taken more than a lifetime to begin to count the stars that were visible to the naked human eye. And a gentle breeze caressed the dark pines of the Black Hills, causing an occasional eerie creak as the branches moved against each other.

Around a campfire sat an incongruous pair. Chasing Deer, an ancient Indian, sported jeans, a worn plaid shirt, and cowboy boots, while John was a young man who looked as though he'd just stepped out of a Brooks Brothers ad. A bubbling stream that passed by about 20 yards from them augmented their animated conversation.

Chasing Deer: John, we have talked much of the day about the differences between your world and mine and of prophecies relating to both. Nighttime, however, has always been for stories, ever since I was a little boy. So why don't we take a break from what your people would call "heavy stuff," and I will tell you some stories of my people. If you listen carefully, you will learn as much about us as from the more heady things we have talked about. How's that with you?

John: I would really love that, Grandfather. I've always thought that in a people's stories you get a glimpse of their soul, if you will. They give a culture flesh and bones. But let me go brew us some coffee first—I have the feeling that we won't be hitting the sack for some time!

Chasing Deer: You're probably right. I can be a talkative old buzzard!

When John returned with the steaming brew, Chasing Deer began.

Chasing Deer: I think that I'll first tell you the stories of some of our Native American cultural heroes. I imagine that you learned something about cultural heroes at Dartmouth, didn't you, Grandson?

John: Of course I did. I didn't sleep the entire time I was there . . . just most of the time! You know, Grandfather, it seems to me that in all cultures there are mythological tales of those exceptional people who are seen as giving the culture both its form and its direction. Their stories express the social, political, and religious values of their society, although not necessarily *all* of these different aspects of the culture. In my Western culture, we have such stories as that of Osiris, Isis, and Horus from ancient Babylonia; but perhaps the most well known are about Odysseus from ancient Greece and Lancelot and the Knights of the Round Table from medieval England. One of my favorites is the story of Roland from medieval France, and there are many others that I remember from my Literary Foundations course. I imagine that almost every culture has such heroes.

There are also real people who might be thought of as cultural heroes in our society. These individuals came to their people in a time of need and gave them new direction and spiritual underpinnings. Sometimes they were political or intellectual figures like Thomas Jefferson or Socrates, but more often than not they were spiritual or religious leaders, such as Moses, Jesus, Mohammed, and perhaps, more recently, Martin Luther King, Jr. As time goes by, I feel that these heroes become persons of mythological proportion, and it's sometimes difficult to sort out the truth from the myth. Well, whatever the case, they do represent the epitome of a culture's values, whether secular or spiritual.

Chasing Deer: Yes, that's the idea. Now, since you have had a fine education, tell me: Have you ever been told of the cultural heroes who lived years ago in what is now called the United States?

John: Do you mean Indians like Sitting Bull, Geronimo, Crazy Horse, or Osceola?

Chasing Deer: Not exactly. The men that you mentioned were all great war leaders and, in the case of Sitting Bull, a great medicine man as well. And, of course, Crazy Horse was a profound mystic. In my estimation, he was one of the greatest men to ever walk upon Turtle Island. Someday I will tell the story of Our Strange Man, as he was known to us, but it will take a week or more.

No, I am talking about the men and women who gave us our religions and our way of life.

John: It's a little embarrassing, Grandfather, but in truth, I don't know of them.

Chasing Deer: No need for embarrassment—believe me, you are not alone. There are few in the United States who know of our cultural heroes. After all, your people are not indigenous to our country, and your educational system teaches you little of the people who occupied this land for at least 100,000 years, if the *Walam Olum* is correct.

John: What's that?

Chasing Deer: The *Walam Olum* is the oldest book in America. It has been passed down for untold generations of Lenni Lenape, or the Delaware Indians, and was recorded on what one might call bark tablets. It tells of the peopling of this continent, which, by the way, did not occur by the crossing of the Bering Strait during the Ice Age.

John: Now wait a minute, Grandfather, that's not what I learned in anthropology class. If the American Indians didn't come here from Siberia, then where *did* they come from?

Chasing Deer: I think that we were always here except for the natives of the far Northwest. It seems to me that an Eskimo looks like a Mongolian, while a Cherokee does not and a Lakota does not—nor, for that matter, does any other tribe that is not from up around the Arctic Circle. Furthermore, Siberian people are about evenly distributed among A, O, and B blood types, yet in pre-Columbian America, all Native Americans were either A or O—yet there was only type-O all the way from the end of the Artic glaciers to Tierra del Fuego. Now get your anthropologist to tell me how a recessive gene that came across the Bering Strait is to this day 97-percent dominant among the natives of Tierra del Fuego at the tip of South America?

John: You might just be right, Grandfather. The Human Genome Project has shown that polygenism is just as logically sound as monogenism—in other words, human beings could have arisen in more than one place. Furthermore, now that I think about it, I remember reading recently that if the Native American arose anywhere but here it was in what used to be called Eurasia, where Europe and Asia meet, so to speak.

Chasing Deer: I don't know about all those big words, but I do know that my People did not come across the Bering Strait any more than they came from the moon!

In any case, the current American people know little of our cultural heroes. This is not so much the case with the cultural heroes of Mesoamerica and South America, for the people there are far more in touch with their ancestral, indigenous roots.

John: Yes, I noticed that in my travels to Mexico and Central America, I often heard ordinary people of indigenous descent talking about such people as Quetzalcoatl.

Chasing Deer: Quite right, and like Quetzalcoatl, many of our cultural heroes were real flesh-and-blood people.

Now, there is one very distinct difference between the roles played by our cultural heroes versus Euro-Americans. Native Americans traditionally have greatly respected wisdom and spiritual values, which is perhaps why Joseph Campbell called us the most spiritual people on Earth. On the other hand, sad to say, Euro-Americans have not given wisdom and spiritual matters the central position in their culture, as it should be. Instead, they have placed more value on knowledge, possessions, and power.

In our culture, when a person of great spiritual depth spoke, they were listened to and taken quite seriously. In your culture, these people have at best been given lip service. I am in no way saying that our spiritual leaders were any wiser than yours, only that yours have not been followed with anything approaching integrity, nor have your people walked the paths that they have been shown. For example, in our spiritual traditions (and in yours), it is wrong to lie, but as you know, the history of the United States is replete with lies, fraud, and deceptive dealings.

John: I am painfully aware of that—and it isn't getting any better. The saddest part to me is that the American people aren't more aware of it. This makes it very hard for a democracy to function at its best.

Chasing Deer: It surely does. In my grandfather's day, lying was considered such a crime against the People that one could be put to death for it. It was considered worse than murder, for it both infected and affected the entire community negatively. People living communally cannot afford for there to be any mistrust among them.

John: That's for sure—the entire fabric of society would break down.

Chasing Deer: Before we get to the story I want to tell you, I think that it would be good for you to understand some of the great differences between your people and mine. Imagine, John, the following conversation that could have occurred several centuries ago between an Indian chief and the Pope:

> Chief: Your Holiness, in the Jewish people's Old Testament, Moses wrote down on a stone tablet the Instructions that the Great Mysterious wanted the Jewish people to follow. One of them says, "Thou shalt not kill." Your people, the Catholics, along with other Christians believe this Old Testament to be the word of God. I have been taught that this is the same God Who is the Father of Jesus. Jesus also taught that one should not kill, that one should turn the other cheek, and that one should forgive seventy times seven. Why then have you and your predecessors condoned, encouraged, and, indeed, been the driving force behind so many wars? Why did you have Inquisitions? Why did you kill millions in the so-called New World in the name of Jesus? And why are you continuing to do so?

> Pope: It is not so easy, my child. Jesus also said, "Render unto Caesar that which is Caesar's" and that includes the right to wage war. You must remember that there is a difference between the secular and the sacred.

> Chief: I have never seen any difference, your Holiness. A tree is just as much a part of the Creator's Creation as I am. When I lead my People, I am responsible to do so by the Instructions given our People by the Creator. Do you mean to tell me that the State or a Caesar can take moral precedence over the Creator's Instructions? That makes no sense to me! The Creator does not talk with a forked tongue.

You have great power, your Holiness. Why do you not make killing in a war what you call a cardinal sin? Just think of all the lives that could have been saved over the centuries and in the future!

Pope: Well, people have the right to defend themselves against aggression. Your people certainly have.

Chief: I agree with you—people do have a right to defend themselves against aggression. So why not make it a cardinal sin to fight an aggressive or offensive war?

This conversation could continue for a long, long time, Grandson. I know—I have had them with the Black Robes when I was a young man on the reservation. Our chiefs could never separate the sacred from any other aspect of life, whereas Christian leaders seem to be forever afraid to morally confront the secular rulers by taking a moral stance for the salvation of their people.

John: What you say, Grandfather, is unfortunate but true. I remember thinking when I was a little boy, *How can my father be part of the planning of the invasion of East Timor, yet go to church every Sunday and listen to sermons on Jesus' mercy and sense of justice?* The East Timor invasion ended up being even a larger genocide than the Jewish Holocaust in terms of percentage of the total population, yet few Americans even know about the slaughter. I was shocked when, in his autobiography, Daniel Patrick Moynihan, then ambassador to the United Nations, told of his role in the massacre. He says outright that it was his job to render the U.N. ineffective in interfering with the United States' plans and to keep the truth from both the American people and the representatives and senators. I find that reprehensible.

Chasing Deer: Yes, being a student of genocide, I know all about it . . . but we are a long way from a story, especially one about a cultural hero! Let's bring this discussion around to focus on the story of Dekanahwideh, which I would like to tell you. If I remember correctly, your family has been involved in the political life of the United States for several generations.

John: That's right.

Chasing Deer: Well, Dekanahwideh was the founder of the Iroquois Confederation, which had quite an influence upon the form of government the United States adopted.

John: I have never heard of him, and I majored in political science in college. What influence did he have upon our government?

Chasing Deer: Since you asked, I will give you a brief history lesson that you probably never learned in school. The story may be of even greater interest to you once you know these things.

As I said, Dekanahwideh founded the Iroquois Confederation, and by doing so, conceived and brought into being the first democracy, or I should say republic, in North America. It was a democracy far richer than that of ancient Greece, for everyone was included in one way or another—no one was considered disenfranchised. Even the early democracy of the United States excluded many from participating in the governing process, including women, slaves, and those who were not landowners. The democracy of the Iroquois was all-inclusive, maybe not in the same way as the modern United States is, but in ways that perhaps checked the willful abuse of power and "cronyism" so common in American government. It also gave women a far greater say in the destinies of their children.

John: When did this take place, Grandfather?

Chasing Deer: The exact dates of Dekanahwideh's life are not known. Iroquoian oral history has him living early in the 10th Century C.E. However, if one uses astronomical and genealogical data, then the confederacy itself was not founded until 1145 C.E. Some anthropologists have a different take, claiming that the confederacy was not established until the latter part of the 16th century. I, however, find the argument of these anthropologists weak, as is often the case when dealing with Native America. They claim that the confederation was formed in response to the growing European presence—yet Indians were far too tribal and individualistic to think like that in the 16th century. Their argument is weakened all the more by the fact that European contact with the Iroquoian nations had been minimal, and really posed little or no threat at that time. It seems that, from all the studies done and when cultural bias is dismissed, Dekanahwideh lived from approximately 1100 C.E. to about 1150 C.E.

John: Wow! That was more than six centuries before the United States was even founded. I've got to hear more about this.

Chasing Deer: Yes, it was quite a long time ago . . . yet the confederation is still intact. Like most cultural heroes, Dekanahwideh's life seems to have been embellished with myth over time. I will leave it up to you, Grandson, to decide where to draw the line between fact and fiction. I only ask that you try to be open-minded. Most of your people dismiss anything Native American that deals with the miraculous as myth, or chicanery. I always tell people that if they wish to dismiss our treasured history as myth then they have to have the logical consistency to do the same with Moses, Jesus, and any number of saints and prophets from Judaism and Christianity. If a person cannot, then they have learned something very important: firsthand experience of cultural bias.

John: Yes, I know—every culture and every religion seems to believe that only *its* stories are "gospel." From our earlier discussion, I learned that this wasn't so with the various Indian tribes. They saw no reason why the Creator *wouldn't* tell different stories to different people, since each tribe's culture and, in particular, its land, was different. So why would an Apache living in the desert have the same creation story as a Mohawk living in the deep forest?

I also find it fascinating that there were never any Indian religious wars, as they were, and are, rampant in my world.

Chasing Deer: Someday, perhaps, I will take you to one of our *Yuwipi* ceremonies, where you will see the Spirits, hear them talk, and feel the rush of a cold wind as they depart—things that are quite normal to us, but miraculous to your people. Your entire perspective on what is will be radically altered, I promise you.

John: Now that's something I'd like to experience! You're not pulling my leg are you, Grandfather?

Chasing Deer: I am a great leg-puller, if you will, but never about the Spirits or our spiritual life. It is *Wakan,* Sacred. Now let's get back to history.

It was as early as 1677 that the British colonists began to consult the Haudenosaunee, the real name of the Iroquois, about how to establish coordination and unity among the various colonies. In 1727, Cadwallader Colden published his *History of the Five Nations,* which was widely read in both colonial America and England. It generated even more interest in just how the Iroquois governed themselves, uniting, ultimately, six distinct tribes along with two others under their protection. This was unheard of in European history.

There was obviously much interaction between the colonists and the Iroquois during the entire colonial period. As time went by, the colonists became very interested in the workings of the Iroquois Confederation, both in terms of curiosity and because of the practical need for a union of some sort among the colonies.

In 1744, the English colonies were seeking advice from the Iroquois on how to deal with King George II and the power structures of the English Empire. On July 4 of that year, Canasatego, the chief of the Onondaga [one of the six nations that composed the confederacy, which was originally five until the Tuscarora joined the confederacy in the early 18th century] offered the following advice to the British colonists:

> We heartily recommend union and a good agreement between you, our brethren. Never disagree, but preserve a strict friendship for one another, and thereby you, as well as we, will become stronger. Our wise forefathers established union and amity between the Five Nations; this has made us formidable; this has given us great weight and authority with our neighboring Nations. We are a powerful confederacy; and, by your observing the same methods our wise forefathers have taken, you will acquire fresh strength and power; therefore, whatever befalls you, never fall out one with another.

Dekanahwideh

The colonies were still unable to act in any concerted fashion. Even though they had learned so much from the Iroquois, they were unable to emulate them. This highly annoyed Benjamin Franklin. In either 1750 or 1751 (historians are unclear as to the exact date), Franklin wrote a letter of dissatisfaction with this state of affairs to James Parker. In part, it says:

> It would be a very strange Thing, if six Nations of ignorant Savages should be capable of forming a Scheme for such a Union, and be able to execute it in such a Manner, as that has subsisted Ages, and appears indissoluble; and yet that a like Union should be impracticable for ten or a Dozen English Colonies, to whom it is more necessary, and must be more advantageous; and who cannot be supposed to want an equal Understanding of their Interests.

Notice the cultural bias here. Even though the Iroquois had been able to accomplish what the Euro-Americans to this day have not, they were still "ignorant savages."

Let me give you an idea of how Iroquoian society functioned under "The Great Tree of Peace" that was established by Dekanahwideh. Again I will read you something from Benjamin Franklin:

> The Indian Men, when young, are Hunters and Warriors; when old, Counselors; for all their Government is by the Counsel or Advice of the Sages; there is no Force, there are no Prisons, no Officers to compel Obedience,

or inflict Punishment. Hence they generally study Oratory: the best Speaker having the most influence. The Indian Women till the Ground, dress the Food, nurse and bring up the Children, and preserve and hand down to Posterity the Memory of Public Transactions. . . .

Having frequent Occasions to hold public Councils, they have acquired great Order and Decency in conducting them. The old Men sit in the foremost Ranks, the Warriors in the next, and the Women and Children in the hindmost. The Business of the Women is to take exact notice of what passes, imprint it in their Memories, for they have no Writing, and communicate it to their Children. They are the records of the Council, and they preserve [the] Tradition of the Stipulations in Treaties a hundred Years back, which when we compare them with our Writings we always find exact. He that would speak, rises. The rest observe a profound Silence. When he has finished and sits down, they leave him five or six Minutes to recollect, that if he has omitted any thing he intended to say, or has anything to add, he may rise again and deliver it. To interrupt another, even in common Conversation, is reckoned highly indecent. How different it is from the Conduct of a polite British House of Commons, where scarce a day passes without some Confusion that makes the Speaker hoarse in calling order; and how different from the mode of Conversation in many polite Companies of Europe, where if you do not deliver your sentence with great Rapidity, you are cut off in the middle of it by the impatient Loquacity of those you converse with, & never suffer'd to finish it.

Dekanahwideh

John: Boy, that doesn't sound like a group of "savages" to me! With all his intelligence and education, I find it hard to believe that Franklin could have written what you just read me and still refer to the Iroquois in the next breath as "savages." It really points out how strong cultural bias can be, doesn't it, Grandfather?

Chasing Deer: It surely does. But do not think that my People, or any others for that matter, are free of it. It is almost impossible to break the chains of culture, which is why we need spiritual practices to bring us in touch with the universally human. We all bleed red!

That's enough history. Are you ready for the story, or do you want more coffee first?

John: No, thanks. You have roused my curiosity—I really want to hear about Dekanahwideh.

Chasing Deer: Good. Here goes.

The Mission of Dekanahwideh

Near the Bay of Quinte long ago, there lived an Indian woman with her young daughter (we do not know her name). The daughter had always been of impeccable character. She stayed at home to learn the ways of her People, and was very close to her mother and a source of great pride to her. When this young maiden entered womanhood, she refrained from all contact with the men of the tribe as much as was possible. Even though she was extremely beautiful, she accepted no suitors. Yet despite her refraining from all manner of activity with men, it soon became clear that she was with child.

How can this be? her mother thought with great distress. She approached her daughter, saying, "My daughter, I am going to ask you one question and I want nothing but the full truth: How can it be that you are with child?"

"Mother, in truth I cannot tell you," replied her daughter.

"This I do not believe, and my grief is great. It is even greater because what you have told me cannot be the truth," her mother answered.

"But my dearest mother, I *have* told you the truth. I do not know how I come to be with child. I have not been with any man," the daughter pleaded.

The sorrowful mother replied, "No, my daughter, you have lied to me, and worse still, you can have no love for me." She was in such anguish that she withdrew from her daughter and became unkind to her. Even so, as the time for the birth drew near, the saddened mother had a dream in which an unfamiliar man appeared to assuage her grief. This is what he said:

"I am here to deliver you a message. I ask you to cease your grieving and the ill treatment of your daughter because it is indeed true that she does not know how she became with child. I will tell you what has happened. It is the wish of the Creator that she bear a male child, who shall be

named Dekanahwideh. This child shall reveal to all men the Good Tidings of Peace and Power from Heaven. Then the Great Peace shall rule and govern on Earth. So I charge that you and your daughter be kind to him, and when he grows up to be a man, do not prevent him from leaving home."

When the mother awoke, she went straight to her daughter and begged for her forgiveness. Shortly thereafter, the baby boy was born, and his grandmother gave him the name she had heard in her dream.

Soon the infant became a young man. Early one morning, he came to his mother and grandmother and told them that the time had come for him to leave for the East. "First, I must build a canoe, and do so quickly, for I leave on the morrow," he said.

It was no ordinary birch-bark canoe that Dekanahwideh began to build; no, he began to chisel a vessel out of a large white rock. When he was done, he went to the women and said, "I must leave now. My canoe is ready. I shall be gone for a long, long time, and may not ever return."

As his mother and grandmother helped Dekanahwideh pull his canoe to the lake, his grandmother exclaimed, "But your canoe is made of stone—it cannot possibly carry you on your journey! It will sink to the bottom as soon as you put it in the lake."

"Yes, my grandmother, so you would think. But this white stone canoe that floats as birch upon the waters shall be the first sign of something wondrous that men shall see." And with that, Dekanahwideh left his mother and grandmother on the shores of the lake and quickly disappeared from view.

Dekanahwideh made his way to what is today called Lake Ontario. There, a group of hunters were camping on the southern side, and one of them had gone down to the shore. As he stood there, the hunter saw the white canoe coming toward him. When Dekanahwideh reached the bank, he climbed out and strolled up to the lone man. "What are you doing here by the banks of the lake?" he asked.

"Why, we are here for two reasons. Obviously, we are hunting; but there is also great unrest and troubled times in our village," the man answered.

"I tell you, go back to your village. You will find the trouble gone and the unrest calm. Tell the chief that the Good Tidings of Peace and Power have arrived. If he asks you how so, then you must tell him that the messenger of these things shall visit him shortly," said Dekanahwideh.

"May I ask who tells me such things?" the hunter requested.

"I am Dekanahwideh, and I come from the West and am traveling ever eastward," Dekanahwideh answered. He then boarded his stone canoe and left.

In awe and wonder, the hunter left for his camp and told the other hunters of his encounter. Upon hearing the story, the entire group left for their home village. When they arrived, they went immediately to the chief and told him what had happened on the banks of the river. The chief wanted to know when these Good Tidings of Peace and Power were coming to his people. The hunters knew only that it would be soon. The chief then decided that the entire village should wait in silence for Dekanahwideh to arrive.

Meanwhile, Dekanahwideh continued his journey until he came to the home of a great and evil wizard, who was called Thadodahho. Many years before, he had left his own people and now lived alone. It was said that Thadodahho was a cannibal, and that any man who came near his domain put his life in great danger. Even the birds avoided flying directly over his home, for they would plunge to the earth dead—such was Thadodahho's power.

When Dekanahwideh saw this evil wizard, Thadodahho was carrying a dead human into his house and then went to the river for a bucket of water. Dekanahwideh crept over to his house and climbed up on the roof so that he could look down the smokehole. He saw the wizard return to cook his meal of human parts. Dekanahwideh heard him say to himself, "Ah, I guess I had best have my dinner and then attend to my other affairs."

Dekanahwideh was curious and moved himself directly over the smokehole to have a better look. Directly below was the kettle with its steaming meat. When Thadodahho went to get himself another piece of meat, he saw the reflection of Dekanahwideh's face staring at him from the kettle. The wizard backed away and sat down to reflect upon what he had just seen. Now, wizards are strange men, and his conclusion was that a face in a kettle was a most wondrous thing!

The wizard thought more and more and at last said to himself, "Hmm . . . how could this be if my way of living is correct and worthy? Could it be that my way in the world is not a good way? I had best go and have another look."

When he looked into the kettle a second time, there was the same face looking at him. And not just any face, but the face of a great man as the wizard perceived it. He picked up the kettle, went far from the house, and emptied it completely.

While the wizard was emptying his kettle, Dekanahwideh hastened off the roof and ran to where he would meet Thadodahho coming back to the house. As they met, Dekanahwideh asked him, "Tell me, what are you doing?"

The wizard replied, "I had put my kettle on to cook a meal, and when I went to take some meat from it, I saw a man's face staring at me. For as long as I have lived, that has never happened before. This led me to think that I must have been living my life in the wrong way. So I carried my kettle over there by the tree stump and emptied it. But where have you come from? You are not familiar to me."

Dekanahwideh said, "I am from the West, but now I travel to the East."

"And what is your name?" the wizard asked.

"In this world I am called Dekanahwideh. And you, where do you come from?"

"I had a village, but I left it many, many years ago," said Thadodahho.

To this, Dekanahwideh responded, "You have become aware of your mistaken ways and forsaken them. Both peace and friendship have returned to your heart, so it is that you must go back to your village and spread this among your people. I will return to you soon."

Then Dekanahwideh traveled on to the house of Djikon-sahseh, who was from the Neuter tribe. Her house was just to the east of Niagara—this was a most dangerous path, for on it traveled many men thirsty for war and destruction. When these aggressive warriors traveled the path, they would stop by her house and she would feed them.

After Dekanahwideh greeted her, he said, "You must cease forever feeding those who go about seeking destruction and death. The Good Tidings of Peace and Power have come. You cannot do as you have in the past. From this time forward, you shall be the guardian of the Good Tidings. Now I charge you to go east to a place of great danger, Onondaga. I shall meet you there in three days, and we shall put all things in order. Now I must continue my journey."

As Dekanahwideh continued along, he came upon a large encampment where he asked to be led to the chief. Once he reached him, he asked, "Have you heard the news that the Good Tidings of Peace and Power are coming to the land?"

"Indeed," replied the chief, "I have heard this from others."

"May I ask what you think of such a thing?" Dekanahwideh continued.

"My mind has been upon this news so much that I have not slept for days," answered the chief.

"The time is now at hand, and you shall be sleepless no more," Dekanahwideh told him. "Furthermore, I shall now give you a new name, and it shall be Hayonhwatha."[1]

Then the chief asked, "Who are you to tell me such things?"

"In this world, I am called Dekanahwideh, and I come from the West. I journey eastward to spread the Good Tidings of Peace and Power, so that warfare and the shedding of blood may be stopped and peace may return to the land," he replied.

"I must go and tell my other chiefs of this good news. Can you wait until I return?" asked Hayonhwatha.

"Yes. Since I see that you are on a mission to help spread the news, I will wait," Dekanahwideh answered.

Hayonhwatha told all the other chiefs to gather the people, for there was a messenger that he wished them all

---

[1] This is the Hiawatha made famous by Longfellow's poem.

to hear. When the people had assembled, he called forth Dekanahwideh.

"The Good Tidings of Peace and Power have come to the land," said Dekanahwideh to all the people, "and it is I who have been chosen to tell you that the Creator wishes that no human should shed another's blood; rather, we all should live in peace."

Hayonhwatha then arose and addressed his people: "Tell me, my brothers and sisters, what you think of that which this man Dekanahwideh has told you? Should we accept these Good Tidings of Peace and Power?"

A warrior chief stood up, a man who was greatly respected and the protector of his people. "To our east are the Mohawk and Oneida people, who seem always to be hostile to us," he said, "and to our west we have the same trouble with the Cayuga and the Seneca. How are we to live with this much hostility?"

Dekanahwideh rose and answered, "These nations have accepted the Good Tidings of Peace and Power. There is no need to fear them now."

"I find this hard to believe," argued the warrior chief. "Listen, my people, perhaps we are being tricked. Do we truly know this man? We need some proof of what he says; we need some proof of his power. Let us ask him to climb the tall tree over there by the cliff, to the very top, and then we shall cut the tree down. If he remains alive after such a fall, then I shall believe him and his power."

Dekanahwideh replied, "In these times of bloodshed, it is wise to be cautious. I will gladly do what you ask. It is because the Good News of Peace and Power has come that I have no fear of placing myself in your hands."

So Dekanahwideh and the people went to the tall tree by the cliff. When they arrived, the warrior chief said, "If by the light of morning you are still alive, then the people shall know of your power, and I will take your message into my heart."

Dekanahwideh agreed. He then climbed the tree, singing the six songs of the pacification hymn. When he reached an uppermost branch and seated himself, the warriors chopped down the tree, and over the steep cliff tumbled both the tree and Dekanahwideh, right into the Mohawk River.

The villagers watched where Dekanahwideh had fallen, but there was no sign of him at all. Finally, the warrior chief said, "We shall keep a close watch for him at the rise of the sun tomorrow. Then we shall know the truth of this man. Now let us return to the village."

When the new dawn came, the warriors went to the cliff where Dekanahwideh had fallen into the river. One of them observed smoke rising from a fire by a nearby cornfield. Cautiously he went toward it, and there was Dekanahwideh, sitting there warming himself. Immediately the warrior returned to the village to report what he had seen to Hayonhwatha.

"Hayonhwatha," he said, "over by the cornfield there sits a man warming himself by a fire. It is the very same man who fell into the river, I am sure."

"Go report this to all the chiefs and to the people. Tell them to assemble here," Hayonhwatha directed.

When the people had gathered, Hayonhwatha asked the warrior chief and his sub-chief to go to the fire and bring back Dekanahwideh.

The two warriors went to the cornfield straight away. They were amazed to see that Dekanahwideh was neither wet nor harmed in any way.

"Would you come with us to the home of Hayonhwatha?" they asked.

"I shall, for this is right," Dekanahwideh answered.

At the home of Hayonhwatha, they counseled for only a brief period before Hayonhwatha said, "Dekanahwideh, I accept the Good Tidings of Peace and Power. It is my word, and I am now bound." He then turned to his warrior chief and said, "The man Dekanahwideh has returned unharmed from over the cliff. I cannot decide for you, for that is not our way, but tell me, what is you opinion now on this matter at hand?"

The chief warrior responded, "My chief, I was in great doubt when this man came. For these many years it has been both my duty and my honor to protect our people. I am the one who asked Dekanahwideh to set himself upon the tree and to have it felled. My honor allows me no choice but to accept him and the Good News of Peace and Power. This is the right and noble thing to do."

"Good," said Hayonhwatha. "Now go in good faith and see to it that what we have decided is known to all the people. This is a time of great rejoicing!"

Then Hayonhwatha turned to Dekanahwideh and said, "You have heard our answer. Both my warrior chief and I agree, and so shall our people. This is all we can say. We know not your plans, so this matter of establishing these Good Tidings rests with you."

"The sun has just arisen, the day is young—so, too, the new and hopeful mind is arising, so, too, are the Good Tidings of Peace and Power. As with the sun, the Good News will proceed on its proper course and the new way of thinking will go forth and prosper. These Tidings shall prevail among our people, and generations to come may live in peace with one another," said Dekanahwideh.

"You, warrior chief," he continued. "Your power shall no longer be in war, but in peace. And I shall give you a new name, Degaihohke, which means 'he who has doubts when choosing between two things.' I must now resume my travels east. We shall meet again soon."

Thus, Dekanahwideh left Hayonhwatha and continued his travels.

Hayonhwatha and Dekanahwideh Spread the Good News

Shortly after Dekanahwideh left that village, a series of misfortunes struck Hayonhwatha. First, the eldest of his three daughters became ill and died. Hayonhwatha fell into a great despondency. His many friends and family members gathered to console him and pleaded with him to drop his sorrow. There was so much work to be done now that the Great News was about the land, so Hayonhwatha laid aside his sorrow, as he knew he must. Yet it was not long before his second daughter became ill and also died. This time Hayonhwatha was inconsolable, despite the efforts of his chiefs and the people. His sorrow was so deep that he could only grieve.

Degaihohke told his warriors, "We must do something to cheer our chief. His trouble is great, and we must help him. I would ask that you consider playing a game of lacrosse. Perhaps this would cheer him, as he loves the game so."

His sub-chief replied, "It is my mind that Hayonhwatha has only one daughter left, and he must be lonely and sad. He needs his People. I say we gather all the People and bring them to console our good chief that he may know how much he is loved."

Degaihohke thought for a moment and said, "I concur with that. The chief needs to feel the love of his People. We must call them all to come and give him words of consolation and strength."

And so the People came. But Hayonhwatha did not answer them, so deep was his grief. The warriors then gathered and began a game of lacrosse, hoping to cheer him. During the game, his last remaining daughter left the family home to go to the spring for water. She was not far from the house when over her flew the most beautiful of birds. It was the *Ha'goks,* which was often called the wampum eagle. Being somewhat scared by the appearance of such a spirit bird, she cried out, "Look, look at this most beautiful of birds!" Then she ran away.

The warriors, hearing her cry, also saw the *Ha'goks* flying low, and they ran after it to see it more closely. So enthralled were they with the sight of the bird that they did not even notice the daughter as they ran following the eagle. The poor young woman was trampled to death, and only then was it noticed that she was with child.

When Hayonhwatha was told what had happened, he cried out, "Oh! Now I have lost my last daughter and my grandchild as well! I cannot stay here. I must travel west to assuage my grief." And he left immediately.

As Hayonhwatha walked along the trail in anguish, he came upon Dekanahwideh.

"There is danger on this trail, especially so because of a man who is currently watching all who come this way," Dekanahwideh told him. "The man is waiting up the trail from you, but he does not yet know that you are here. It is most important that you get to him before he becomes aware of you. If you can do so, it will be a good omen for our mission. If you succeed in this, ask him what it is that he is waiting and watching for. He will tell you that he is looking for strangers from other tribes and for wild animals, because he is protecting the cornfields of his tribe so that the children may eat."

With this warning in mind, Hayonhwatha traveled on. Not far down the trail, he saw the man looking over the cornfields. Following his warning, Hayonhwatha made sure that he approached unnoticed. While the man was facing away, Hayonhwatha quickly walked up and asked, "What are you doing here?"

The startled man replied, "I am guarding the cornfields from other tribes and from wild animals so that there will be plenty for our children to eat."

"You must leave now and go tell your chief that the Good Tidings of Peace and Power have come," Hayonhwatha told him.

The man instantly got up and left. When he got to his village, he told his chief that the Good News of Peace and Power had come.

"Who told you such a thing?" the chief asked.

"I was guarding the cornfields when all of a sudden this man appeared beside me and told me to bring this news to you," replied the man.

Meanwhile, Hayonhwatha had gone to the end of the cornfield where he met Dekanahwideh.

Dekanahwideh told Hayonhwatha, "This is good. The news has been delivered. Now you shall stay in this hut and wait for them to come back to you. Make some wampum from elderberry twigs. A woman shall come by early in the morning, and she will notice you and return to the village to tell the chief. In due time, the chief will send a messenger to get you, but you are to go with no one until you are brought wampum similar to what you have made. This is important. Now I must go."

Hayonhwatha found the hut, built a fire, and waited until morning. As the dawn broke, a young woman came out to get some fresh corn for her children. She saw the smoke from the fire and walked to the end of the cornfield. Seeing Hayonhwatha, she turned immediately for home and went to the chief's lodgings. "My chief, when I went to the cornfield, I saw a strange man sitting by a fire in front of the old hut. I have never seen him before," she reported.

"What was this man doing?" questioned the chief.

"He was sitting there with his head hung low, as if he were muttering to himself," she replied.

"He seems to be no threat," the chief said. "It must be the man who sent back our guard with what he called the Good Tidings of Peace and Power. I shall send a messenger to get him."

The messenger went on to the cornfield and found Hayonhwatha looking intently at the elderberry twig wampum he had made. Three times he asked Hayonhwatha to come to the village, but received no response. So he left and returned to the village. When he got back to the chief, the messenger said, "The man made no reply to my request that he come with me to the village. Three times I asked him, but he uttered not a word."

"Tell me, what did you see there?" asked the chief.

"The man was sitting staring at a long string of elderberry twigs that he had hanging on a pole in front of him," the messenger replied.

"Ah," said the chief, "now I understand. He needs for me to send him a similar token of wampum in assurance that we both intend to meet in peace. I will make two strings from quills and hang them together. It is the wampum that needs to speak to him, not your words. This time, both you and my warrior sub-chief will go to the man."

Dekanahwideh

Shortly afterwards, the two warrior chiefs left for the cornfield with the chief's finely made quill-wampum strings. When they arrived at Hayonhwatha's fire, the warrior chief said, "Our chief has sent us to you once more, but this time he sends these fine quill wampum as his message that you should come to him."

"Good. That is how it should be. These are fine quills. As soon as I have finished my smoke, I shall come to your village," Hayonhwatha said.[2]

The two warriors left him and returned to the chief's home. When they arrived, they told the chief that the man had responded that he would come as soon as he had finished smoking.

"Good," the chief said. "Go tell the people that I want them to assemble here so that all may hear what this man has to say."

In due time, Hayonhwatha arrived. The people were all assembled at the home of the chief, who came forward and said, "It seems from what I have heard that you have come to tell us something of great importance. I have assembled all my people so that they may hear what you have to say. This way, there can be no misunderstanding among us. It is our way. We are ready to listen when you are ready to speak."

"Thank you, my chief. I have come to you and your people to deliver a message, a message of the Good Tidings of

---

[2] For a Native American to leave for anything of importance without deliberating with himself first is considered insulting to the other party.

Peace and Power. I come with this message that your children and their children may live in peace."

The chief answered Hayonhwatha, saying, "We cannot answer you now. We are waiting for a man to return to us. When he comes, we shall deliberate. Meanwhile, it is our desire that you accept our hospitality and stay in our village with us. It is my understanding that this man should be back before too long."

"I shall stay as you ask and await this man," answered Hayonhwatha.

"This is good. It may be that the man who is coming has the same message as you. I shall see to it myself that you are taken care of and that your stay with us shall be most pleasurable," the chief said.

"This seems to be as it should," replied Hayonhwatha, and he was led to his quarters.

That night, he had no sooner lain down and closed his eyes when he heard a voice outside his room asking, "Is this where you are staying for a while?"

He replied that it was, and was told to come outside immediately. There he found Dekanahwideh.

"Hayonhwatha," he said, "It is important that you leave now. We both must journey. All that can be done here has been done for the present."

As they sat beneath a large elm pondering how to proceed, they heard a voice saying, "It has yet to occur."

Startled from his deliberations, Dekanahwideh said, "We must go to the place from which that voice comes."

They had not traveled far when they came upon a beautiful lake. Dekanahwideh said, "The man with the voice we heard lives beside this lake. I am going to leave it to you, Hayonhwatha, to decide what we should do. There are two ways to get across the lake: We can take the boat that you see over there, or I can have us float by magical means over to the other side. I must warn you that the man who lives on the other side has been known to tip over a boat if he sees it coming, and many people have drowned. Which option do you prefer?"

Hayonhwatha answered, "I think that the wiser course is to float over the lake, but we must do so in such a way that when we are on the other side we can approach the man from behind. I sense that he has been waiting impatiently—to approach him directly may be asking for trouble."

So Dekanahwideh had them magically float over the lake and arrive at some distance behind the man. He was sitting on a knoll, and Hayonhwatha approached from his left side and Dekanahwideh from his right. As they neared, he was still calling out "I have yet to see it occur!"

Soon they were by his side, but still unnoticed. Then Hayonhwatha saw what the man was doing: Every time he called out, the lake became rough with waves that surely would have capsized a boat.

Dekanahwideh then spoke: "I promised you I would return with a man you have never seen. I have kept my promise, and we are here."

The man turned around, surprised that Dekanahwideh had been able to come upon him unnoticed. "Who is this new man that you have brought with you? Where is he? And what is his name?"

Dekanahwideh replied, "Turn to your left and you will see."

When the man turned and saw Hayonhwatha, he asked brusquely, "What are you doing here?"

"I am here, standing beside you, because our hearts and our minds are with you. This is so because the Good Tidings of Peace and Power are now upon us. If you will turn and look all about, you will see smoke arising from many settlements and encampments. In each of them there is peace . . . and also peace with their neighbors," said Hayonhwatha.

Suspiciously, the man stood and looked slowly all about him. When he saw the smoke arising from so many different places, he asked, "Who will see to it that these Good Tidings that you talk of will be sent forth across the land? Who can accomplish such a thing?"

Dekanahwideh answered, "Sometime tomorrow the representatives of the various settlements will come here to you. It is then when they arrive that all things will be done."

The doubtful man then said, "I shall stay here and await them."

Now both Dekanahwideh and Hayonhwatha traveled to the village where Hayonhwatha had stayed at the chief's lodge. When they arrived, Dekanahwideh called for the chief to come out. When the chief saw that Hayonhwatha had returned, he was grateful, and he invited him into his home, where he said that the man he had been waiting for had returned to the village. "So, since the man has returned, we can now give our answer to your Good Tidings," he added.

"I am ready to hear your answer. My companion is with me," said Hayonhwatha.

"Then bring him in!" the chief said.

When Dekanahwideh came into the chief's lodge and seated himself, the chief spoke to both of them: "Our man has returned and given us the message of the Good Tidings in a way that we fully understand what it means. It is the same as you have told us; therefore, we accept your offer."

Dekanahwideh arose and said, "Let us then conclude everything. Who was the first among your tribe to hear of the Good Tidings of Peace and Power?"

"It was the man who was guarding the cornfield," the chief answered.

"Can you bring him here to be with us?" asked Dekanah-wideh.

The chief called in a warrior and asked him to go and find the man in question. In a short time he was back with another warrior, and the chief said, "This is the man who was guarding our cornfield that day."

"Are you indeed the man to whom Hayonhwatha came? What is your power in guarding the cornfield?" asked Dekanahwideh.

The warrior replied, "I am that man. My power is in my bow and my arrows."

"Tell me," asked Dekanahwideh, "how is it that you carry your power with you?"

The warrior answered, "My arrows I place in my quiver, which I carry on my back."

"Then from this day forward, you shall be called Ohdahtshedeh, the quiver bearer. Now that the Good Tidings of Peace and Power are upon us, you shall no longer be the guardian of the cornfield, but rather the guardian of the children, that they may live in peace," said Dekanahwideh. "And now, my chief, where is the man for whom you have been waiting?"

The chief called for the man to come to his lodge, and Dekanahwideh verified that he was indeed the man for whom the people and the chief had been waiting. "Tell me," he said, "what was the cause of your delay?"

"There was another man who came by our village," he replied. "He had promised to return but had not. I had gone out to meet him on the path, and I waited a long time for him. Finally I began the trip home to the village. But I could not find the trail. What had been a clear path was now a forest. When I eventually got back here, I found that the people had heard of the Good Tidings of Peace and Power from Hayonhwatha. It was this news that I was to bring to them."

"All is well—you have done your duty," said Dekanahwideh. "But now your duty has changed. You shall spread the Good Tidings of Peace and Power throughout the land so that the generations to come may not know warfare and destruction. I tell you all, I have traveled through many villages across the land, and all the people have accepted the Good News. The time has now come for Hayonhwatha to return to his own people, and I must go far to the village atop the big mountain. I have received no answer from these people. The Great Peace must be concluded. We all need to work together. Two among you must go and find villages that have yet to hear the Good News."

Hayonhwatha then asked, "Now that we are all going our separate ways, where is it that we shall gather again?"

"My canoe lies at the mouth of the Oswego River. It is there that we shall meet," replied Dekanahwideh.

Next, Ohdahtshedeh spoke: "I shall wait at my village, and when you come to me, I shall accompany you. I shall also find two men to go and look for villages that have yet to hear the Good News." He looked toward his gathered warriors and asked, "Which two of you shall take upon themselves this most important mission?"

"I will," said the warrior chief. "Now I need one volunteer to go by my side."

There was no answer. Ohdahtshedeh asked again, and there arose not a voice.

"I shall ask one last time. Who will go on this mission with our warrior chief? If you will, speak now!" Ohdahtshedeh demanded.

"I will go on this mission," said a voice from afar.

"Where is that man?" asked Dekanahwideh.

When Ohdahtshedeh called in the man, he was asked to stand beside the warrior chief.

Then Dekanahwideh told him, "It was good that you came from outside of our meeting to volunteer. I am making you the assistant to the warrior chief, and it shall be your duty to perform all that he commands that pertains to our mission. Now go in search of those villages that have yet to hear the message of Good Tidings of Peace and Power. When you arrive at a village, go immediately to the chief and tell him the Great Message. Say that chiefs have sent you and that you have come to lead them to a conference. They are to send delegates from their villages. When you are asked where the meeting is to take place, tell them it is by the lake where the Mighty Wizard lives, the one with the booming voice. They will know where I mean."

The members of the gathering left to go perform their respective missions, and Dekanahwideh and Hayonhwatha left for their home villages.

When Hayonhwatha arrived back home, he told his people that they were now to go to the conference. "I ask you to prepare for a journey and that we may leave as soon as possible," he said. When the two volunteers from Ohdaht-shedeh's village left, the people saw them transformed into hawks. They took off southward, and when they arrived at the settlements of the Cayuga, they were again transformed into men. At the village, they asked to be taken to the chief, whom they told about the Great Meeting.

"In truth, I have known of this for some time," said the chief. "Furthermore, I know the message that you bring, and I accept it, so you know my intent is peaceful. When I finish smoking my pipe, I shall go."

Their mission accomplished, the warrior chief and his companion returned to their village, where Ohdahtshedeh asked them, "Did you find the village?"

"Yes, we did," they replied. "When we arrived, we found the chief outside his lodge smoking. So we knew that he was in deliberation with himself. He told us that he had already heard the Good News and that he would attend the conference."

"Hayonhwatha should be coming soon, and when he does, we shall all depart," said Ohdahtshedeh.

Meanwhile, Dekanahwideh had gone to the village at the top of the great mountain. When he arrived, he went to the lodge of the chief.

"The time is at hand," he told the chief. "I need your answer to the message that I left with you some time ago."

"Unfortunately, we cannot reach agreement in the tribe. Both the warrior chief and his sub-chief do not agree with me on this matter. They do not think that we should accept the Good Tidings. I cannot think of a way to over-come their objections, for they both have more control over the people than I do. After all, it is these two who have defended the people all these many years," the chief replied.

"Do not worry about this. You are the chief and have accepted the Good Message. Come with us to the conference, and there you will see that you are far from alone. Perhaps the many good minds there can help you with your difficulty," Dekanahwideh said. "And now, I would ask you to go to the other settlement of your people across the river. Tell them to come to us now, for it is most important that we all meet as soon as possible."

The chief dispatched his fastest runner to his brother chief's lodge across the river. It was not long before they both arrived back. The group held a council, and when they were done, Dekanahwideh asked, "Now that we have met in council, I need to know your minds. Can you tell me?"

The chief from across the river answered, "My chiefs and I have become of one mind. We accept your offer. However, we have the same problem as our brother chief here. Our warrior chief and his sub-chief oppose us."

"I understand," said Dekanahwideh. "But I still encourage you to come with us. At the great council you will meet many who have accepted the Good Tidings. Now I shall give you both new names. You shall be Skanyadahriyoh and your brother chief, Sadenkaronhyes. This is now well and good."

Then Dekanahwideh left the village upon the mountain. Upon the way he came across Ohdahtshedeh, who said, "We were growing impatient, as for some time we have heard the man by the lake calling."

"Go now," said Dekanahwideh. "I must first go to my lodge. I shall meet all of you where we agreed."

The Conversion of Thadodahho and the Formation of the Council

Dekanahwideh was the first to arrive at the appointed place. Shortly thereafter, Hayonhwatha, Ohdahtshedeh, and the chiefs they had gathered arrived. Not long behind were Skanyadahriyoh and the chiefs who accompanied him.

When all the chiefs, sub-chiefs, and others had assembled, Dekanahwideh arose and said, "I am glad that you have come. We have here four nations assembled and shall not wait for our mother, Djikonsahseh. The first thing we should do is cross over the lake. The rulers with power shall cross first. Come now, Hayonhwatha, Ohdahtshedeh, Dyonyonko, Skanyadahriyoh, and Sadenkaronhyes. If these rulers can get across the lake and make peace, then all the others may cross over. Watch closely, for you will see a great display of power when they cross. Hayonhwatha, you are to guide the boat."

Dekanahwideh entered the white stone boat and went to the bow. The other chiefs followed him, with Hayonhwatha coming last and sitting in the stern. As it embarked, from the distant shore they heard a loud voice summoning them, saying, *"Asohkekne—eh,"* which means, "it is not yet." No sooner had the voice rang out than a powerful wind arose, making the lake rough and troubled. Waves higher than any of them had ever seen careened across the lake and surrounded the boat. The chiefs in the boat were caught in a whirlwind of fear and shouted, "Now is the time we are all going to die!"

Dekanahwideh reassured them, saying, "There is no danger because peace has prevailed upon the land. Gaha, my Wind God, you may rest and be still."

As quickly as the turbulence had started, it ceased. But that was short-lived. The man across the lake again called out in a voice such as only a giant could command: "*Asohkekne—eh,*" and the great wind and troubled waters arose again.

Once more, Dekanahwideh commanded the Wind God, "Be still, we have yet to cross!" And again the lake became placid and smooth.

With the lake calmed, Hayonhwatha began to paddle with great strength, and when the shore was reached, the boat skidded up and buried its hull in the land. Such was Hayonhwatha's power.

The chiefs followed Dekanahwideh up a short path where they beheld a man sitting upon a grassy knoll. Dekanahwideh led them toward him, and when they arrived, the chiefs all stood in a circle around him with Dekanahwideh directly in front of him.

"I have come back as I promised," Dekanahwideh said. "Here with me are the representatives of four nations. I ask you now to answer the message that was left for you. Each and every one of the chiefs that stand around you has accepted the Good Tidings of Peace and Power. With this acceptance, the shedding of human blood shall cease forever among them. They have recognized that our Creator does not want human beings engaged in the destruction of one another, and the same holds true for all nations. As you look out over your lake, think of all the men who have perished before your eyes. These chiefs have come to ask you to join them. The destruction and warfare must stop; the Good Tidings of Peace and Power must prevail, that our children might live without fear and in prosperity."

The man cast his gaze upon each chief, but he would not answer. They all noticed that his hair was moving, slowly writhing as if each strand were a snake. When they looked at his hands, they saw that his fingers were continually twisting this way and that.

After a long time, Dekanahwideh told Hayonhwatha, "Go back across the water and bring back the warrior chiefs and our mother, Djikonsahseh."

The ride across the lake was smooth and calm. The new arrivals climbed the path to where the silent man was sitting, and when they arrived, Hayonhwatha said, "It is done. We now have everyone assembled and in agreement."

Dekanahwideh then addressed them all: "Let us begin by giving thanks to the Creator that we have been able to complete this mission. Each nation represented here shall have voice in our thanksgiving. I shall start out: *'Yo—hen!'* [Thank you, it is good.]"

Each chief in his turn repeated, *"Yo—hen!"*

Then Dekanahwideh addressed the man sitting by himself. As he spoke, the man became ill at ease; he was soon so affected that he began to shed tears. "We have brought together all the nations and their chiefs who have accepted the Good Tidings of Peace and Power. It is now time for a representative of each nation to speak his truth about what we are trying to achieve and to address this man before us who will not accede to our mission."

The first to speak was Ohdahtshedeh, who said, "I think it is most important that this man approve our goals of peace and unity. Perhaps he may give approval if each of us would lay our heads before him. By this, I mean that our nations would be subordinate to him."

Dekanahwideh and Skanyadahriyoh said, "We will agree to do as Ohdahtshedeh asks."

"Thadodahho," said Dekanahwideh, "tell me, are you satisfied now that these chiefs have offered to lay their heads at your feet?"

Thadodahho still would not answer.

Dekanahwideh continued, "All right then. Dyonyonko, it is your time to speak your heart."

Dyonyonko then spoke to Thadodahho. "My heart tells me that the Creator brought this day to us. There is a new light upon our Earth and upon our faces. Thadodahho, look around you—here are the representatives of four powerful nations, the warrior chiefs, and Djikonsahseh, our mother. We have all given our approval and our hearts to the Good Tidings. We have all offered you the Good News, and we have offered to make you the Fire-Keeper of the Confederate Council. Your nation shall be in the center, and we offer ourselves as subject to you."

As he spoke, the chiefs noticed that the writhing of Thadodahho's fingers and the serpentlike movement of his hair gradually ceased. At last he spoke: "I, Thadodahho, will now answer you. I do accept the words that you have brought to me. I fully take into my heart the Good Tidings of Peace and Power."

Upon hearing this, Dekanahwideh said, "We have now done all that the Creator has desired of us except one thing: We need to transform this man. We shall do that by giving him a rubdown, cutting off his hair, and circumcising him."

The chiefs did all that Dekanahwideh asked. When they were done, Thadodahho seemed more like other men and not so much like a monster.

Then Dekanahwideh said, "It is now time to place a set of antlers upon each other. We shall use deer antlers because it is deer that feeds us. The antlers are symbols of your authority as chiefs, and they give you the power to rule your people."

And this was done, one chief to another.

Upon the ground next to Dekanahwideh lay one more pair of exquisite buck antlers. These he asked the warriors chiefs and the mother to pick up and place upon the head of Thadodahho. When they were done, Dekanahwideh said, "Arise, Thadodahho. Behold, you chiefs, this man who stands before us. The buck's antlers have been placed upon him. They are the symbol of his authority. From this time forward, all people shall call him Chief Thadodahho. And forevermore, when we, the United Nations, create a chief, we shall all gather in ceremony to mark the occasion."

Then he suggested that the clans take one another as brothers and cousins, and the chiefs answered in one voice,

"Your suggestion is a good one, and we are all in favor of adopting it."

So Hayonhwatha named his colleagues, and his nation was called Mohawk. Then Ohdahtshedeh founded the Oneida nation, and similarly the Seneca and Cayuga were formed.

Now only Thadodahho was left to name his brothers and cousins. When he had done so, Dekanahwideh said, "Thadodahho, your tribe shall be called the Onondaga, and forever shall they sit at the center of all council fires. Now the chiefs and representatives of the Confederacy of the Five Nations have been named. The chiefs have all been adorned with antlers. The foundation of the confederacy is complete."

He and the chiefs all smoked their pipes, and when they were done, Dekanahwideh rose to speak again. "We need to address the fact that the chief warriors of the Seneca so far have refused to adopt the Good Tidings of Peace and Power," he announced. "This is so, even though all the chiefs gathered here have given it their approval and their hearts."

The chiefs agreed that this was troublesome to them, and they sent messengers to the Seneca warrior chiefs to come to the council. When they arrived, Hayonhwatha said, "All of the chiefs and their many warriors gathered here have accepted the Good Tidings. You are the only ones who have not agreed. We would like you to tell us your thinking on this most important matter. But before you speak, it is important for you to know that the chiefs in this Council and all their warriors have decided unanimously to give to the Seneca warrior chiefs, full power in all things related to the waging of war in defense of this confederacy."

The elder of the two warrior chiefs then stood and addressed the Council: "My chiefs, my fellow warrior chief and I have decided to accept the Good Tidings. You have our sacred pledge."

Next, it was Dekanahwideh's turn to address the Council. "This is good," he said. "All now seems complete, and we must add these two chiefs to our Confederate Council. Our confederacy we shall call *Kanastahgekowah,* meaning 'the great black door' through which all messages must pass, both good and evil, if they are to come before our Council. If any nation or any person has business to bring before the Council, or any messages, they must now pass through this door.

"My chiefs," he continued, "let us now crown these two warrior chiefs with antlers, that they may be fully equal to all the other chiefs here gathered. From this time on, they shall be cousins and guardians of the door of the long house. Let us now lay the slippery bark of the elm tree upon the entrance floor. When someone from a foreign nation comes to our council lodge, the two doorkeepers shall escort them so that they do not fall; but if someone comes to us with evil intentions, he shall slip upon the floor and his nation be conquered, after which we, in council, shall decide what to do with him."

The Laws of the Confederacy

Dekanahwideh then began to establish the Laws of the Confederacy. This is what he said to the gathered chiefs:

"Now that we have all come together, and the Good Tidings of Peace and Power have been accepted and the Confederation of the Five Nations has been agreed upon, we must establish the laws of our Confederation. First of all, there shall come a time when vacancies shall occur in our council and we will have to select new members to fill them. A vacancy shall occur only by death or removal. Those who are chosen to fill such vacancies must come from the same clans and the same families as the previous chief. Thus, the title of chief, insofar as the council is concerned, shall be hereditary. I hereby name the women to take this duty of naming a successor. If there is a vacancy, the women of the chief's clan shall name the new chief.

"Let us now make a council fire. The smoke from it shall arise, and all the nations that see it shall know that we are one. Since you sit in the center of our council, Thado-dahho, you and your relatives shall have the responsibility to care for and protect the fire. Also, before you shall be laid *Skanodahkenrahkowah* and *Kayahrenhkowah,* our great white wampum belts. And before your feet shall be laid this great wing. It shall be your duty, and that of your relatives, that should any evil ever fall upon the great wampum belt, you must take this wing and dust it clean.

"Furthermore, this rod shall be laid before you. If you notice anything that could harm either our grandchildren or the great white wampum belt that represents the Great Peace, you are to take this rod and drive it away. If, despite your efforts and those of your brothers and cousins, you cannot drive away such evil, you must send word out to all the confederate nations that they may come and help you.

"Now, my chiefs, let me show you where you should sit before the council fire. The Mohawks and the Seneca shall sit on one side of the fire, and on the other side, opposite them, shall sit their sons the Cayuga and the Oneida. All matters will be handled under the precepts of the Great Peace, and the great white wampum belt should make you ever mindful of where your heart and mind should be in your deliberations.

"Thadodahho, as the Fire-Keeper of the Confederate Council, you shall open all meetings. Be sure at the opening of each meeting to give both praise and thanksgiving to the Creator for the Great Peace that has been brought to the Five Nations. When you close a meeting, you should again give praise and thanksgiving.

"Once the council has been opened, it shall be Hayonhwatha and his Mohawk brothers who will first consider the matter at hand. When their deliberations are over, they shall give their opinion to the entire council. Next it will be the turn of the Senecas to give the matter at hand their full consideration. When they reach a decision, they will refer it back to Hayonhwatha and his Mohawk brothers. It shall be Hayonhwatha's responsibility to convey the decisions of both the Mohawk and the Seneca to the Oneida. Then Ohdahtshedeh and his Oneida brothers shall consider and deliberate upon the matter. When they have made their decision, they will refer to their brothers the Cayuga. As soon as the Cayuga arrive at a decision, they shall give it to Ohdahtshedeh, and he shall announce the Oneida and Cayuga joint decision to the Seneca and the Mohawk.

"It shall then be Hayonhwatha's responsibility to refer the matter to Thadodahho and his brother Onondagas. They shall carefully consider the decision of the others, applying the principles and the spirit of the Great Peace in their deliberations. Should they not be satisfied that the matter has been properly considered or the decision not reflect as fully as possible the spirit of the Great Peace, they shall refer it back to the two sides of the council fire for further deliberation. It shall now be fully reconsidered until Thadodahho and his brothers believe that it is in accord with the Great Peace and can be confirmed.

"Should the Mohawk and Seneca be unable to agree, then Hayonhwatha shall give both decisions to the Oneida and the Cayuga. If they, too, should disagree, then Ohdahtshedeh shall give notice of this to the opposite side of the council fire. Then Hayonhwatha shall refer the two decisions to Thadodahho, who, together with his brothers, shall decide which alternative is most in accord with the Great Peace. In the case of there being four separate decisions, Hayonhwatha shall refer them all to Thadodahho, and the choice shall be left entirely to him and his brothers, and their choice shall be final.

"The manner in which the Confederate Council of the Great Peace shall conduct its business is now set," said Dekanahwideh.

"There is still much to do, however," he continued. "Each nation shall adopt whatever is put forth here. The decisions shall then be carried forth to our villages and adopted there. In this way, the message of the Good Tidings of Peace and Prosperity shall be carried out and fulfilled among our various people, and we shall secure for them peace and happiness and assure that our grandchildren shall live free of any conflict or war between us.

"When you return to your respective nations, this is how it shall be. Each of you council members shall assume the same role in your nation that Thadodahho assumes among you; that is, all discussions and decisions shall be given to you for your approval or disapproval.

"Now we have finished setting up national councils, and we have the means whereby we can govern our respective nations. The capital of the Five Nations Confederacy shall be in Thadodahho's village, among his nation, the Onondaga."

With this business done, Dekanahwideh said, "Let us now go and plant a tree. We shall plant a tall-standing, powerful tree, and we shall name it The Tree of the Great Long Leaves. Once it is planted, it shall grow long white roots that shall extend to the North, the South, the East, and the West. On top of this tree, we shall place the great bird whose vision is long and powerful, the eagle, so that he may watch the roots and see if any evil is coming toward the confederacy from any of the four directions. Should it see any evil approaching us, it shall screech and screech until the confederacy is gathered to ward it off. Under this tree, our business will be transacted. It shall stand as a symbol for the Great Peace and for the Good Tidings of Peace and Power. The many nations of the Earth shall see it and stand in awe. They will seek the tree by following its roots and, thus, arrive here where we plant it this day. When any nation arrives here in this manner, you must welcome them and allow them a seat in our confederacy.

"As we no longer stand alone, let us combine all our individual power. Then we shall have the power of one great confederacy. Each nation shall contribute one arrow, symbolizing that nation's power. We will combine all the arrows into one great bundle, and when thus tied together there will be nothing that can break it. Our union as brother nations will be complete with the tying of these arrows into one bundle. We must remember our commitment to the Great Tidings of Peace and Power and to the Great Peace that we have now attained. If any arrow is lost, the bundle becomes weaker, and the more it may lose, the weaker it will become. The confederacy must maintain its strength, or all of us will suffer and our grandchildren will live with the constant danger of war."[3]

Dekanahwideh's address continued: "To tie our separate arrows into one bundle, we shall use the sinew of a deer, for it is strong and durable. Thus shall this confederacy be both strong and durable. All the chiefs, all the warriors, and

---

[3] The back of the United States dollar bill shows an eagle holding a bundle of arrows. The symbolism was "borrowed" from the Five Nations Confederacy.

all the women are now united. This bundle shall reside under the Great Tree, and when we council, it shall stay by Thadodahho's council fire. From this moment forth, all the peoples of the Five Nations shall have one heart, one mind, and one body. This is now done.

"Now my chiefs, together we shall stand in a circle holding hands. Should a tree fall upon our circle, our combined strength shall be such that our grips cannot be broken. Inside the great circle of chiefs, our people and our generations to come shall live in peace, security, and happiness.

"Should it be that any chief wearing the deer horns pull from this circle or harm it, then his horns shall be fastened to our circle and the chief matron will warn him. If he continues in ways that may harm the circle, then his horns shall be permanently attached to the circle and he will no longer be a chief or a member of this council. Furthermore, from that time forward he shall not be allowed to fill any office or position in the confederacy except that of warrior.

"Now we must consider what to do as far as disposing of the weapons of war collected from the people of the Five Nations."

The chiefs considered this weighty issue under the rules of decision-making that Dekanahwideh had established. When they had come to a unanimous decision, Thadodahho told Dekanahwideh, "We all agree that the best thing to do would be to remove the Great Tree for the moment and deposit all the weapons in the cavity that shall be revealed. The stream far below the Great Tree will carry the weapons quickly away to be seen no more so that these means of harm and destruction will never have to be viewed by our grandchildren."

Thus, the Great Tree was uprooted and the weapons cast in the chasm to be seen no more. Then the tree was replaced and secured as if it had never been uprooted.

"This is good," said Dekanahwideh. "Now we must address the matter of the hunting ground of the people."

When the chiefs had duly considered the matter, they said, "We have decided that as we are now all one people, the hunting grounds of the Five Nations shall be open to all, for if we kept our national hunting grounds as they are today, it could be a cause for bloodshed when one crossed into the land of another. So, in the spirit of the Great Peace, we think that what we have decided is best for all."

Now Dekanahwideh said, "The Confederacy of the Five Nations has been formed, and the ways in which business shall be conducted has been established. It is time for me to leave all other matters in your hands. Always remember that you are to work for the good of all—do not vary from the guidelines and principles that I have given you. The welfare of the people must come first. I now place all power in your hands. You are free to augment whatever I have given you, for things will become clearer in time and things change with time, but all must be done according to the spirit and the principles of the Good Tidings of Peace and Power. I place upon you the responsibility of never seriously disagreeing with one another. The council is no place for quarreling, as each of you has equal power, and there is no distinction between chiefs. It is during quarreling that the white panther of disharmony and discord appears. This should never happen, or you will lose all that has been gained and your grandchildren shall suffer. Always keep your hearts open and remember that you are all brothers and cousins.

"Should this ill ever happen, then whichever one of you can climb the highest tree must do so and survey everything that he can, to see if there is any way to overcome this situation and leave it behind. If he can see no way out of the dilemma, then he must come down from the tree. Look then for the greatest swamp elm that you can find and gather there, all of you, and put your heads together for a solution from the heart, one that is guided by the Good Tidings of Peace and Power.

"Should you fail in this, all shall suffer henceforth. Perhaps you will have to leave and go westward with your heads rolling. It will be that other nations will see you leaving and your rolling heads and they will say, 'You were once a proud and noble people, you people of the confederacy. Look at you now.' They will scornfully kick your heads and leave you there. Yet they shall regret doing this, for there will be enough pride residing in your memories that you will avenge yourselves upon them.

"And there may be other troubles. As the roots of our Great Tree go in all directions, it may be that other nations try to harm these roots. If this happens, it will be very troublesome, and your place of council will become uneasy and restless. I tell you now that when trouble comes, your skin must have the thickness of the span of your thumb to your little finger. This I charge each and every one of you to have—it must be so. No matter how disturbing or burdensome anything that comes before your council may be, you must have patience, you must not let aggravation overcome your good will, and you must never give in to the disgrace of anger. No matter how serious, no matter how troublesome your considerations and your deliberations, you must always, no matter what, be forever guided by the Good Tidings of Peace and Power. This is the only way that you will be truly successful.

"I ask you, my chiefs, with all the earnestness at your command, to develop and nurture only those feelings that are good and binding between you. Friendship, love, and honor must be cultivated among you.

"I believe that I have done all I can in helping you," Dekanahwideh concluded. "If you will be diligent in your duties to the Great Peace, then what we have created here will last from generation to generation for as long as the sun comes up to bring the day."

"However, if at any time you are remiss in your duties and the people begin to suffer in any way because of it, I shall return. Should it ever be that my name is spoken disparagingly or in jest, or in disrespect without good cause, then you may know that great trouble is not far off. My name should be mentioned only in the ceremony of condolence or when the Good Tidings of Peace and Power are being learned or discussed for good and noble purpose."

The chiefs told him, "We shall begin our duties and carry them out in the manner that you taught us."

Then they continued among themselves: "We have begun with our Five Nations. It is our hope that other nations shall also accept the Good Tidings and put themselves under the Great Law of the Confederacy. If they do, they shall be as strong trees supporting our long house. All shall be welcome.

"Let us make the great white wampum belt represent our council fire. When the Fire-Keeper opens our council, he should hold it up high as he gives thanksgiving to the Creator. Then it shall rest in a place where all can see it. When we are finished, the Fire-Keeper should again pick it up and hold it high while saying a prayer of thanksgiving to the Creator. When we come to the council together, we shall smoke the great peace pipe."

To all that had been said, the chiefs unanimously agreed. Next, they set about to make clear the code of conduct expected of a council member and what to do if that code was violated. "Should a chief willfully commit murder, rape, or thievery," they began, "he shall be stripped of his horns without warning. The horns shall then be given back to the chief matron of his clan and family.

"If a chief obstinately opposes the decisions made in council or the process and insists that it be his will that be carried out, then he shall be called to the chief matron of his family and she shall exhort him to do as he should and strongly urge him to return to the council and live in peace and harmony with his fellow chiefs.

"Should he still insist on his way and not heed the chief matron, then a warrior from his family and clan shall be sent to admonish him and tell him to veer off his evil course, for it will not serve the Five Nations.

"If the chief fails to obey the request of both the chief matron and the warrior, then both shall seek out the warrior chief and present the situation to him. Then the warrior chief shall go to the chief and tell him that he has come for the third time to tell him that he must stop his destructive obstinacy, and that if he does not, then he shall no longer represent either his family or his clan. If he still will not hear the voice of reason and peace, then the chief warrior shall take his antlers from him and return them to the chief matron.

"Should this ever come to pass, then the chief matron of the family and the clan shall choose the chief's successor and place the antlers upon his head, and he shall be the new chief and council member."

The chiefs went on. "Each member of our council shall have one assistant. It shall be the assistant's duty to carry messages for the chief from village to village. It shall also be his responsibility, should the chief be ill or in any way indisposed, to sit in for him in council and have his full authority while in council.

"We are now done with the duties and obligations of the chiefs that sit in our council. It shall be our tradition that when any chief has been deposed for any of the reasons listed above that he may no longer sit in council or be allowed any position of authority among the Five Nations."

The chiefs then moved on to consider other matters. "How," they wondered, "are we to proceed in the case of the death of a chief? There must be some procedure established for the people are dependent upon each and every chief to carry out the business of the nations."

Their answer was this: "If a chief has died, then both the chief matron and the warriors of the family and the clan of the deceased chief shall select a warrior from the family and the clan to replace him. The new man shall be brought before the council, and there his brother chiefs shall decide if he is acceptable as a chief. If they decide that he is, then the matter is submitted to the cousin chiefs. If the cousin chiefs also confirm this man, then he is raised to his new status by the condolence ceremony for the dead chief.

"Should it ever happen that a particular family and clan should cease to be, then the tribe shall consider whom to nominate for the vacancy. The successor must come from a family of brother chiefs to the chief who is departed. The chiefdom shall remain in the family of the man nominated to fulfill the vacancy. However, the council shall have the power to dismiss the new chief if it is not content with the manner in which he is fulfilling his obligations and select a chief from a different family.

"Further, should it ever be the case that the chief matron of a family or of a clan shall die and there is no one to replace her because there are only male children left in that family or clan, then the chiefs of the nation of the departed matron may select, from a sister family, a female of age to select a temporary matron from that sister family. However, when a woman reaches matronhood from the original family or clan then she shall replace the temporary matron from the sister family."

The chiefs, having finished with the regulations and the means for implementing them, then moved on to consider the actual implementation of these regulations and means. They decided that in each of the villages of the confederacy, they would look for a warrior of the highest character and wisdom that was dedicated to the well-being of his people. Should he be willing to dedicate himself to service for the people, then the chiefs shall appoint him to aid them in the carrying out of the regulations and means in his village. He shall be given the title of "He Who Has Sprung Up As a Pine Tree." This title shall not be hereditary, but will die with him.

The chiefs continued their deliberation on the rules and regulations of the confederacy, saying, "We have chosen all our chiefs and they have been seated in their respective places, but what should happen if there is a death among us before we again meet in council?"

They agreed to the following: "What we will do is this: While the chief is still dying, we shall go to his lodge and remove his antlers and place them beside him. If it be the Creator's will that he recover from his illness, then we shall replace the antlers of his power. He may then, when he recovers, continue with his duties as a chief. Also, during his illness, we will go and put by the head of his bed a string of black wampum. Should he die, then any member of his clan may come and take the black wampum string and come forward and tell the confederacy of his departure. He must do this as follows: If the chief that has died be a member of the three brother nations—the Mohawk, the Seneca, or the Onondaga—then the black wampum shall be taken to a son of the three brothers; that is, either Ohdatshedeh or Dekaehyonh, or if they are unavailable, then the black string of wampum shall be left with one of the son's colleagues. As soon as he leaves the house of the dead chief on his mission he shall, as he goes along, cry the mourning cry, *Kwa—ah, Kwa—ah, Kwa—ah.*

"When Ohdahtshedeh or Dehkaehyonh or their colleagues have received the black wampum, they shall take it to their four brothers, and this shall continue from brother to brother until the entire confederacy has knowledge that the chief has departed. Now, if there is a death among the two brothers, the Oneida and the Cayuga, then either the warrior chief or any other warrior must take the black wampum string to Dekarihoken or Skanyadahriyon or Thadodahho, or, if they are not available, to one of their colleagues. He, too, shall cry the mourning cry, *Kwa—ah, Kwa—ah, Kwa—ah* all along his journey.

"It may also be that a warrior chief dies from the center or either side of our council fire; if that happens, then the warrior carrying the message shall only repeat the mourning cry twice.[4]

"When a chief dies suddenly, then his friends shall take off his antlers and put them aside until the chief matron comes and takes them to her lodge.

---

[4] This was also done later on for the warrior chiefs of the tribes adopted into the confederacy (but not members of the council)—the Delaware, and my tribe, the Nanticoke. In the early 1700s, the Tuscarora became the sixth member nation of The Great Confederacy.

"We will also do this if a chief among us dies. We shall erect a pole with a pouch hanging at the top, and in that pouch there shall be a small string of wampum. This shall be done by the side of the council fire where the dead chief sat. A member of the other side of the council fire will then take the pouch of wampum from the pole and go to the other side, and before the fire console them with well-chosen words. After his consolation has been offered, he will cheer them so that their grief may abate. When the condolence ceremony is held, there shall be present 11 strings of wampum, and there shall be spoken 11 passages from the condolence ceremony ritual."[5]

John: I'm amazed, Grandfather, that the obvious impact of the Iroquois Confederacy was never mentioned in any of my courses, especially in my American history and Constitution classes. The influence is obvious, and Franklin's writing put the matter beyond question.

Chasing Deer: Unfortunately, history is often written to please the culture, not the truth.

John: So I'm beginning to learn!

---

[5] There are other narratives related to the founding of the Confederacy of the Five Nations, which can be found in Arthur C. Parker's *Parker on the Iroquois,* from which the narrative in this chapter was adapted. Over the years, the laws of the Confederation of the Five Nations have been added to and enlarged, but the laws and the principles in the above narrative remain as they were given.

To this day, more than 850 years later, the Haudonosaunee (the real name of the Iroquois) still meet in council, and for all these years there has never been hostility among them. It is the world's longest-standing republic, yet most Americans are unaware of the great debt that their present form of government owes to these "savages."

CHAPTER TWO

Sweet Medicine

It was another clear and beautiful night. The moon was bright and luminous, and beside the campfire, the shadows of Chasing Deer and John flickered like a psychedelic show. They'd had a late dinner of Chasing Deer's buffalo stew and were now quietly passing his pipe back and forth. When Chasing Deer had taken the last draw, he reclined upon his buffalo robe and began to speak.

Chasing Deer: Well, Grandson, now that we have sent our prayers up the Great Mysterious, are you ready for a story?

John: I was hoping that you'd tell me about another Indian cultural hero.

Chasing Deer: That's exactly what I had in mind. Tonight I will tell you the story of Sweet Medicine. As you know, my mother was Tsististas, or Cheyenne, as the white people call us. Sweet Medicine brought the Cheyenne their religion. How long ago I do not know, but it was many, many centuries ago.

Sweet Medicine was, in my estimation, the greatest of all the prophets of the Plains Indians. For me to tell you the entire story of his long life would take many campfires. So this is an abridged version, if you will.

If you drive to Sturgis, South Dakota, you will find Bear Butte about 12 miles east of the city. You can't miss it, for it rises out of the plains like a giant resting bear. This is the sacred mountain of the Lakota, the Cheyenne, and several other Plains tribes.

On Bear Butte, there is an ancient cave where the Spirit Elders of his tribe instructed Sweet Medicine. The cave is still there, of course, but some years ago the United States Army blew up the entrance, claiming that there was a danger of children wandering into it and getting hurt. I do not believe that one bit. The Holy Mountain is ours by the congressionally ratified Fort Laramie Treaty of 1868. However, the United States has never honored that treaty—in fact, it has not honored *any* of the 371 treaties that it has made with the American Indian tribes. As such, it stands in violation of both international law and its own Constitution.

John: What do you think was the real reason that they closed the entrance to such a sacred cave?

Chasing Deer: As I see it, Grandson, it was due to the ongoing attempt by the United States government to eradicate our religions and our sacred places and turn them into public parks and so forth. You must remember that Indians did not have religious freedom until 1978, under the Indian Freedom of Religion Act. The federal government still does not respect the religious significance of sacred places; consequently, our lawyers are constantly in court fighting to preserve this aspect of our religious heritage.

It is not unlike what happened with the buffalo, which is also sacred to us. In 1874, both the House of Representatives and the Senate passed an act to protect the quickly diminishing buffalo herds. However, on the advice of his generals in the West, President Grant never signed the bill and it became a pocket veto. Then in 1875, General Philip Sheridan, an ardent Indian hater and author of the famous statement: "The only good Indian is a dead one," in a talk before both houses of the Texas legislature said, "[The hide hunters] have done more in the last two years and will do more in the next year to settle the vexed Indian question, than the entire regular Army has done in the last 30 years. They are destroying the Indian's commissary, and it is a well-known fact that an army losing its base of supplies is placed at a great disadvantage. Send them powder and lead, if you will; for the sake of lasting peace, let them kill, skin, and sell until the buffaloes are exterminated."

John: That's dreadful, Grandfather. Why are human beings so vicious?

Chasing Deer: Let us explore that in the morning or we will never get to bed! By the way, Sheridan almost got his wish. There were only 40 known wild buffalo left by the late 1880s, from an estimated 40 *million* prior to the Americans hunting them. But let me tell you about Sweet Medicine now.

Long before the white man came, our People had fallen on bad times both spiritually and morally. I am not sure of the reasons that had brought them to such a state of self-centeredness, and modes of behavior that were so destructive to communal life; nonetheless, it happened. We might even have vanished as a distinct tribe if Sweet Medicine had not come along and restored us as human beings. Here is his tale.

The Story of Sweet Medicine

One night, a young woman still living with her parents had an unusual dream. In it she heard a Spirit voice say, "Sweet Medicine shall come to you." The dream occurred on three successive nights and began to worry the girl. After the fourth occurrence, the young woman told her parents, who made light of the dream and told her to think nothing of it. There must have been something in the dream that disturbed them, for our People do not take dreams lightly.

The dream had spoken true in a way that neither the young woman nor her parents had expected, for the young woman was soon with child. Her parents were filled with embarrassment because their daughter was unwed, so they kept the pregnancy from the tribe.

When the young woman's time came, she went down to the creek alone to have her child in seclusion. She built a small shelter and placed the healthy baby boy within it, hoping to avoid the shame of being found out. Not long after, an old woman went to the creek to gather grasses for the soft bedding they provided. She heard what she thought was a baby crying, but she dismissed it, thinking that it was just other people gathering grasses. But the crying continued, and since no one was in sight, the old woman followed the sound to its source. There she found the abandoned newborn and took him to her tipi to show her old husband. To her surprise, the old man raised his hands to the heavens, proclaiming, "It is our grandson, and we shall name him Sweet Medicine!"

The old couple found a nursing mother, and with her help, raised the baby. He grew quickly into a strong young boy who outstripped the other boys of his age in the tribe. And at the tender age of ten, Sweet Medicine performed his first miracle.

Times were lean for the Cheyenne, food was scarce, and the buffalo were hard to find. So Sweet Medicine went to his grandmother and asked her for a buffalo hide, which he had her prepare according to his instructions. When that was done, he asked her to make a hoop from a cherrywood bough. Next, he asked her to make four pointed cherrywood sticks with forks of one, two, three, and four prongs. When the buffalo skin was properly prepared and cut into one long strip, it was used, along with the hoop, to make a net with a center hole, not unlike a dream catcher.

By this time, the People were wondering what was going on. Sweet Medicine went to the center of the village with his grandmother, taking all the objects that she had made according to his instructions, and the tribe gathered around him in a circle. While his grandmother brought the hoop to the center of the circle, Sweet Medicine laid out his sharpened sticks in a row. When he picked up the first stick, the one with the single fork, his grandmother rolled the hoop crying, "Grandson, here is a yellow buffalo calf," and Sweet Medicine threw the first stick at the rolling hoop. The hoop fell over. Sweet Medicine and his grandmother repeated this with the next two sticks until only the fourth stick was left. When the hoop was rolled the fourth time, Sweet Medicine sent his last stick cleanly through the center hole, and the hoop changed into a young buffalo with an arrow in its side. The People were told to get the meat they needed, which they did until they had their fill.

As this remarkable boy grew, he continued to perform feats that even the most powerful of the Cheyenne medicine carriers could not. From the time Sweet Medicine was a young child, his grandmother had been aware that he often disappeared from the tipi at night. She had no idea where he went or what he was up to, but she knew that he must be going somewhere where he gained extraordinary and powerful medicine.

Not long after his nocturnal disappearances began, Sweet Medicine started to wear a buffalo robe with the hair turned to the outside; and he also carried a soft, downy, white feather from the underside of an eagle's neck. His grandmother noticed that it was these things that seemed to give him the medicine power he had somehow received. He would always don his robe and carry his white eagle feather when he returned from his mysterious journeys. And every time upon his return, he would perform some marvelous feat for the People. His favorite was to make buffalo appear and disappear, and soon the People began to associate Sweet Medicine with this animal. Of course the buffalo was quite sacred to the Cheyenne, as it provided their food, clothing, and shelter, along with scores of other items such as spoons and storage containers. So anyone in the tribe who carried buffalo medicine was seen as very special. Thus, the entire tribe admired Sweet Medicine.

However, as I have said, this was not a good time in Cheyenne history. They had lost their way, and not even the old ones were sure how this had happened. There had been a fading of the moral values for which the Cheyenne were so well known by the time the white man came across them. Chiefs were not becoming chiefs by the tribal acclamation of their generosity and skills—instead, they were like the chief of Sweet Medicine's tribe, Young Wolf. Young Wolf was a man obsessed with power, a trait strongly disliked in later Cheyenne culture and indeed, by all the Plains Indians. Young Wolf and his warrior band ruled by both fear and force. Whereas later chiefs were known for their generosity and the putting of their own needs second to those of the People, Young Wolf took what he wanted.

The People knew that this was no way for a Cheyenne to act, yet they were at a loss as to how to overcome the tyranny of Young Wolf and his henchmen.

The elders gathered and consulted the medicine men and women of their generation. They all remembered the old and correct ways of being Cheyenne, but they could not find a solution to the problem. So the medicine carriers of the tribe tried calling for what is called an incantation dance. During such a dance, medicine men and women take turns dancing and then showing some remarkable feat demonstrating the medicine they carried. The medicine carriers decided to invite Sweet Medicine to see just how powerful *his* medicine was.

The young man was not in the least surprised that he was invited to perform at such a prestigious event. He prepared himself in a correct medicine way, painting his body red and encircling his face, his ankles, and his wrists with black paint. He wore only his worn-out buffalo robe and a yellow eagle feather in his hair, and in his hand he carried strands of sweetgrass. There was one other thing he wore, which no one had ever been known to wear before: a bowstring of buffalo sinew tied around his neck. Thus adorned, Sweet Medicine entered the lodge of the medicine carriers as if it was his rightful place and he had been there many times before.

The elder medicine men welcomed the young man with sincerity and thanked him for coming. Sweet Medicine was given the choice of where he wished to sit, and he sat on the right side of the lodge. The usual feast of roasted buffalo began after he was seated. When all had had their fill, the pipe was smoked to honor the event. Each medicine carrier then took his or her turn dancing, and while doing so, performed the most remarkable of feats, as only medicine people can. Some were able to swallow red-hot coals, others took razor-sharp arrows and passed them all the way through their bodies, and some, with great effort, coughed up stones so large that they should have choked them to death.

As these were powerful medicine people renowned throughout the tribe, many wondered how Sweet Medicine would fare amid so many important shamans. But Sweet Medicine sat unperturbed and quite unassuming while he watched one medicine person after another perform. When it was his turn, the gathered Cheyenne wondered what he could possibly do that would rival what they had already seen.

As the drummers drummed, Sweet Medicine began to move with barely perceptible steps. Slowly he increased the speed and the tempo of his dance, as if carefully building up excitement and expectation among the medicine carriers and the rest of the gathered Cheyenne. As the quickness of his steps increased, Sweet Medicine slowly began to tighten the sinew bowstring about his neck. Soon the veins in his neck were visible; at this point, he handed the ends of the bow-string to two medicine men, telling them to pull the strings tighter and tighter. As they pulled with ever-increasing strength, Sweet Medicine threw his braids of sweetgrass in the fire, fell to his knees, and covered himself from head to foot with his buffalo robe.

In a flash, Sweet Medicine's head rolled on the ground, completely severed from his body by the bowstring. He then lunged forward toward his severed head and sprang to his feet with his body as whole as it ever was! The old medicine carriers were astounded—never had they seen such power at a medicine dance. All proclaimed this incredible display of Sweet Medicine's power. He was, without a doubt, a youth to be reckoned with and respected.

But things did not go smoothly for Sweet Medicine, as is often the case with prophets and holy men. They, too, must learn their lessons and overcome themselves. The difference between them and us is that they persist under greater pain and loneliness than most of us seem to be able to endure. We become the beneficiaries of their wisdom and spiritual struggles. So, here is what happened to Sweet Medicine.

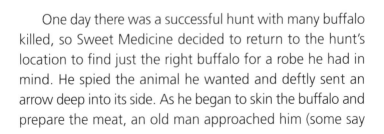

One day there was a successful hunt with many buffalo killed, so Sweet Medicine decided to return to the hunt's location to find just the right buffalo for a robe he had in mind. He spied the animal he wanted and deftly sent an arrow deep into its side. As he began to skin the buffalo and prepare the meat, an old man approached him (some say he was Young Wolf in disguise). The old man said that the hide of this particular animal was exactly what he had been looking for, and he insisted that Sweet Medicine give it to him. Sweet Medicine refused to give up the hide, but offered the old man all of the animal's succulent meat. The old man continued to insist on having the hide, claiming that if it were not given to him he would just take it. Sweet Medicine was finally so overcome with rage that he struck the old man with a severed buffalo foot, knocking him unconscious.

Now there are few transgressions graver than an act of violence against an elder, so the warriors of the tribe set out in search of Sweet Medicine. While they could find his tracks, they could not find *him,* for he was a shape-shifter and could assume the body of an animal. This made him impossible to catch. Finally, after many years, the chiefs asked Sweet Medicine's brother to find him and tell him that he could return to the People. His brother did so, and the two went on a successful buffalo hunt. Yet when the brother returned to the camp for dogs to carry the meat, there were still many who did not want the exiled man back, so his brother abandoned Sweet Medicine and the buffalo on the plains.

Two years later, the People relented, and the brother once again found Sweet Medicine, who was so angry that he would neither talk to his brother nor even look at him. In desperation, his brother sent Sweet Medicine's elderly grandparents to ask him to come home. But it was no use—Sweet Medicine remained silent, and no pleas could reach his heart.

Four years later, while still living away from the tribe, Sweet Medicine came across some young boys gathering rushes and grasses for the People to eat. The buffalo had grown scarce, and Sweet Medicine's People were very hungry. Sweet Medicine asked the boys to get him some bark from the inside of an elm tree. When they returned, the medicine carrier took the bark and turned it into meat for the boys to eat. After they had eaten, Sweet Medicine directed them to take the rest of the meat back to the camp and to tell the People that it was from him.

The tribe had grown weary and hungry during the years that Sweet Medicine was gone. The chief was so grateful to have food for his hungry People that he sent two runners to ask Sweet Medicine to return, but this time he also offered the hand of his daughter in marriage. Sweet Medicine did return, wed the beautiful young woman, and lived for many happy years with the People as they prospered, thanks to his wise counsel and constant care. Yet they were still not the People they used to be. They needed to be revitalized and renewed spiritually.

Sweet Medicine and his wife announced that they were going on a journey and might be gone for a while. It was while traveling to the Black Hills that Sweet Medicine received his Instructions from the Spirit World and was given the Four Sacred Arrows of the Cheyenne.

Sweet Medicine and his wife came across a large butte that rose from the prairie and was shaped just like a Medicine Bear when approached from the West. This was Bear Butte, the sacred mountain of the Lakota, Hidatsa, and other tribes of the area. High up on the butte, Sweet Medicine found a well-hidden cave. With caution he entered, for it could easily have been the den of a mountain lion or a bear. To his utter surprise, the inside of the cave was not what he expected at all, but rather a large, sacred medicine lodge. More surprising, there were people inside, and while they seemed like ordinary folk, they were not. They were not people at all, but Spirits . . . and very powerful ones at that.

Sweet Medicine was immediately welcomed and told that his arrival had been expected—in fact, a place among the Spirit Elders was waiting for him, so he sat down among them. (One can only imagine what it must have been like to be sitting amid such a gathering from the Spirit World!) They told him that their hearts were sad to see such a once-noble tribe so lost and without direction.

"Sweet Medicine," a man as ancient as the stars said, "we are going to teach you what the People have forgotten. When you are done here, you must go back to the People and teach them once again how to live as Cheyenne."

Another Spirit Elder arose, his face and body painted as only the most powerful of Medicine Carriers were allowed. He took the Four Sacred Arrows from a bundle and handed them to Sweet Medicine. And then he said, "Grandson, these Sacred Arrows of long ago will bring the People back to their true ways. These two are for hunting, and these two are for war. Yet that is only the least of their powers— hidden deep within the arrows are the ways and traditions by which the Cheyenne are to live. The Sacred Arrows will renew their bodies, their minds, and most important, their spirits."

The Spirit Elders revealed that they were the 44 greatest chiefs of times long since past. They had hoped that the People could find their own way back to the spiritual laws and traditions that had once made such a noble and honorable tribe. Since they had been unable to, in their compassion and love for their People, the Spirit Elders had to intervene, which was why Sweet Medicine was brought to the cave deep within Bear Butte.

Taking turns, the Spirit Elders taught Sweet Medicine all that he needed to know to carry back to his People for their renewal. He was taught how to care for the Sacred Arrows, how to pray with them, how to renew their power, and how to construct a Sacred Medicine Tipi in which they were to be kept. He was taught all the moral and social precepts that would lead to strength and honor, generosity and courage, trustworthiness and dedication, selflessness and compassion.

He was taught the proper honoring of women, a characteristic for which the later Cheyenne were so well known. (Even today, one will hear a Cheyenne quote Sweet Medicine about womankind: "There is a special magic and holiness about the girl and the woman. They are the bringers of life to the People, and the teachers of the little children." And there is an ancient saying among my mother's people that probably came from Sweet Medicine: "A nation is not conquered until the hearts of its women are on the ground. Only then is it done, no matter how brave its warriors nor how strong its weapons." And among my father's People, the Lakota, there is a similar sentiment which I heard spoken by a very wise friend of my generation to his granddaughter upon her marriage: "The honor of the People lies in the moccasin tracks of the women. Walk the good road. Be dutiful, respectful, gentle, and modest, my daughter. And proud walking. . . . Be strong, with the warm, strong heart of the Earth. No people go down until their women are weak and dishonored, or dead upon the ground. Be strong and sing of the Great Powers, within you, all around you." I mention this only to show you that what Sweet Medicine learned in the Sacred Cave Lodge remains with the People to this day. Now, back to the story.)

Then there were the rules for the warriors to follow so that they might fight with honor and nobility. And so it went, until the Spirit Elders had taught Sweet Medicine about every aspect of right relation and tribal life. And Sweet Medicine was infused with the love and the power of the Creator.

When Sweet Medicine returned to his People, he went to the lodge where the medicine women and men were gathered. He told them that he had been to Bear Butte and that there, in a cave, he had talked and stayed with the Great Mysterious.

The medicine carriers fully remembered the strong medicine that this remarkable individual had carried as a very young man. *How powerful and full of vision he must be now, after communing with the Creator on a most sacred mountain,* they all thought.

Nevertheless, the tribe was still in spiritual disarray—they just could not seem to get back to their old ways. Because there was little food, things were even worse, so the People were not only deteriorating spiritually but physically as well. The medicine carriers knew that they must have a new way or all would be lost for the Cheyenne they had remembered from their long-ago youth. "Sweet Medicine," they cried, "the People are lost! They are all hungry and so weak. Everywhere there is mourning and dissolution. Please, *please* take pity on us. You have been to the Sacred Mountain, and you have spoken with the Creator. You must tell us what to do so that the People may be restored in mind, body, and spirit. Tell us, Sweet Medicine, that the People may live again!"

Sweet Medicine gathered the medicine people around him outside the Medicine Tipi and brought out a bundle that they could all tell was very sacred. He said, "My People, while I was gone these many years, I came across a cave on the Holy Mountain of the Lakota People. Inside the cave were gathered many Spirit Elders, and they gave these to me." At which point Sweet Medicine brought forth his Sacred Bundle, untied it, and showed the People the Four Sacred Arrows.

"The Spirit Elders gave these to me," he continued. "These arrows are most sacred and most powerful. Through their medicine, the tribe can and shall be renewed to our former greatness as a spiritual and loving People. They will not only bring us the buffalo so that we may be nourished and have shelter, but they will also renew our spirits so that we may once again become a good, loving, and strong People. We have forgotten that the most important thing in life is to help one another, and that none are to be excluded."

As Sweet Medicine led them into the Medicine Tipi, everyone could tell that he was indeed a man chosen by the Creator. His very posture and presence commanded the deep respect afforded only the greatest of chiefs and the most venerable of elders.

Once inside, Sweet Medicine told the elders and medicine carriers more of what the Spirit Elders had communicated to him from the Creator: "What has caused our downfall have been selfishness, thoughtlessness, and a lust for power by some—characteristics of a people that the Creator looks upon with disfavor. Somehow, over a few short generations, we have lost our way and our spiritual bearings. These Sacred Arrows will bring us back to a good and honorable path so that we may again thrive and live in harmony with both ourselves and the many tribes that are our neighbors. We have been fighting and arguing among our neighboring tribes and ourselves. The warrior only fights to defend his children, his women, and his elders, so what we have been doing is wrong. It has been based on a selfish drive for power and a forgotten sense of community—without which we are all doomed, for we are only as strong as our community. *All* are grandsons and granddaughters of the Great Creator. This we must never forget. As a tribe, we must go to those we have harmed and offer to smoke the pipe with them in peace so that a new day may start.

"Many of you, it seems, have forgotten to pray every day and to acknowledge the Spirit Beings that surround you; and most important, you have forgotten to rely on the Creator and to approach Him with humility and sincerity. You must not just pray occasionally, but four times a day: You should make good, sincere prayer in the morning when you arise, at the noontime, at the sunset, and before you go to sleep at night. Daily you must seek to increase your conscious contact with the Spirit World and follow, without wavering, the instructions that are given to you by the Above Beings.

"What you have all forgotten is the essence of life, the essence of happiness, the essence of what makes for a healthy and powerful people—and that is service to others. Be aware of what needs to be done for our communal welfare, and when you see such a need, do not wait for another to start the task; instead, take it upon yourself. If you see a job in progress, do not walk by or look the other way, but offer to help. Be especially aware of the needs of the children, the widowed, and the elderly. Bring these people the best part of your buffalo, especially the old and the infirm, as they need the nourishment. Care for these people as you would your own newborn, for it is often hard for them to care for themselves just as it is for a baby. Respect the elders, for without them you would not be here; without them the knowledge that you have would have been lost. Always remember that they are precious, for they hold the memories of who we are as a People.

"As for the children, if a child is orphaned, take her or him into your tipi as if she or he were your own, for we are all of one blood. There are no strangers among the Cheyenne—only mothers and fathers, grandmothers and grandfathers, uncles and aunts, brothers and sisters. We must always be as one. Teach the children from the day they are born to be Cheyenne; that is, to be generous, to live with courage, to live for the good of all, and to always keep present in their hearts the knowledge that they are only as strong as the tribe.

"One thing that you must never do is lie. Lies are worse than murder, for they destroy the spirit, they destroy trust, they destroy community, and, like moths, they eat away at the very fabric of society."

Then Sweet Medicine repeated what he was told in the Sacred Medicine Cave and added this about women, marriage, and family: "The women should remain modest and pure in their hearts, for they are the teachers of the little ones, and how can they teach what they do not themselves possess? The feminine virtues and the purity of the girls and the women must always be protected, and this must be so for all women, whether of our tribe or not—even in warfare, they must be honored. The women should refrain from physical contact with men until they are married. This is important, for all children should be born in love and within the Sacred Circle of Life. If a marriage takes place in the Spirit, then the children will grow to be strong and good, for they will be surrounded by harmony and love, and shall grow to be Cheyenne by the example of their parents. Children learn far more by what they see and hear—by example and by tenderness—than they do by talk. Learning by teaching will only take place if the soil is already properly prepared. This is your duty as a parent and as a grandparent, both to the children and the Tribe, for the children are the future of the Tribe.

"Boys, from the time they are very young, must be shown and taught the greatest respect for girls and women. In their hearts they must recognize them as the sacred beings that they are: the bringers of life, the future, and the strength of the Tribe. They are to be protected at all costs, and they should be looked upon in purity and adoration. As one would never think to defile a beautiful, crystal-clear lake, so should our men look upon our women. They are as our Grandmother Earth: life-giving, selfless, and forever nourishing. With these things in their hearts, both the men and women of the Tribe will have marriages of beauty, children of integrity, and strength of spirit. Do not forget these things, my brothers and sisters.

"Unfortunately, there will be those who will find it difficult to behave and live as Cheyenne. They may do evil things. However, you must forgive them and *keep on* forgiving them, and do all within your power to bring them back to the proper ways of the People. But, only continue to do this if they are willing to makes amends and are truly remorseful. Be sure that they learn to do things that will help the tribe and that they are willing to give all that they have, if need be, to heal any harm that they have done. If you see that they do not do these things and continue to be a threat to the harmony of the People, then warn them that if they continue in this way, they will become outcasts from the tribe. However, warn them only twice, and be sure that they know the full consequences—if you must go to them a third time, they will be banned from the tribe, and should they return, they will be killed on sight. The harmony and peace of the tribe cannot be infected with such evil. Have you not seen in the past what happens when men like Young Wolf are allowed to live among us?"

From that moment on, Sweet Medicine instructed the People about what he had been taught and brought a new ceremonial life to them. Many of the ceremonies that Sweet Medicine created to reinforce and give expression to the Cheyenne way of life are still practiced today.

After a long life of more than 100 years, Sweet Medicine called the tribe to him, for he was greatly troubled and knew that his time on Earth was drawing to a close. He told the gathered tribe that he had given them the instructions that they should live by, and that only if they continued to follow those instructions would they remain strong. But should they fall from those ways, all manner of trouble would beset them. This having been said, Sweet Medicine delivered his famous prophecy. My late friend John Stands in Timber gave me this rendering of it:

There are many people on this Earth besides the Cheyenne and their Indian brothers. At the same time, many people that you know nothing of shall come from the East. Some of them shall be black, but there will be a fair-skinned people, and they shall be numerous.

These fair-skinned ones shall have hair much lighter than yours, and they shall have hair upon their face. Their customs and manners shall be very different from yours. They will come with their own ways of thinking, and they shall not pray to the Great-Grandfathers as you do. Listen to nothing they say. But I fear that, trusting them, you will listen.

These fair-skinned ones are a restless people, and they are never satisfied. They do not know what it is to be content and grateful for all that the Great-Grandfathers and Grandmother Earth have provided. They will move quickly from one place to another, ever pushing forward, and more and more of them shall come. They shall not come to you only on foot, but also in strange things upon the rivers and in boxes upon the land. Their clothing shall not be like yours, but rather made of many pieces together and in many pretty colors.

They shall offer you many things, like isinglass [a reflective object, such as the white man's mirror]. All that they offer you will do you no good and will begin to sap both the strength and the will of the People. Their food shall be strange, and they shall offer you something like sand to eat that shall be very sweet. Eat nothing that they give you, for none of it will be good for you. But worse of all, they will offer you a strange drink, and if you drink it, you will go crazy. Unfortunately, you will like these things that the Earth Men bring, and more than likely you will take them. I warn you that, if you do, your troubles will be never-ending. Take nothing from them. But I fear for you, and my heart is very heavy.

These people will kill the animals and will uproot the Earth. The buffalo will be hunted down for sport. Our four-legged brothers and sisters will begin to disappear. They shall hunt them with a strange and powerful weapon—it shall be noisy, and from it will be sent something like a pebble, which will be deadly.

When they come, they will bring with them their own kind of animal—not like the buffalo, but one with short, shiny hair; white horns; and split hooves. They will eat these animals, and so will you. There is another kind of animal that they shall bring, one with a long tail and hair about its neck. This animal will allow you to travel far. With the coming of this animal, your decline shall begin. That is what I fear.

These people do not love Grandmother Earth as you do. They will dig her up and fly in her air. They may even take lightning from the sky so that where they live they can see at night. Ceaselessly they will search for a certain stone that our Great-Grandfather has placed upon the Earth. They do not follow the ways of the Great-Grandfather, and they will dig and dig into the Earth to find this stone. They will kill our Grandmother Earth.

I see unknown sicknesses coming to you. You will die off—maybe all of you will die. And worst of all, if any of you do survive, these people will want your flesh, the very children of the People. This you must never let happen, for, if you do, your children will become like them, and they will know nothing. These people are restless and will do all in their power to make you like them. They will not stop.

My heart is saddened, for you will not remember what I have said to you—you will leave your religion for something new. You will lose respect for your leaders and start quarreling with one another. You will lose track of your relations and marry women from your own family. You will take after Earth Men's ways and forget the good things by which you have lived, and in the end become worse than crazy.

I am sorry to say these things, but I have seen them, and you will find that they come true.

By most accounts, Sweet Medicine died many hundreds of years ago at Devil's Tower in Wyoming; by others, he began his journey to the Spirit World just west of Bear Butte. No matter which, he ranks as one of the world's great spiritual teachers and prophets.

John: Wow, Grandfather. I don't think that I've ever heard a prophecy that was so clear and straightforward.

Chasing Deer: Yes, all of our prophecies have that kind of clarity. Of course, all of Sweet Medicine's prophecies have come to pass. It only remains to be seen if the white man's ways shall finally kill our Grandmother Earth and all her children. It is certainly true that many people are awakening to the multifaceted ecological problems now facing the Earth and her children, and many brave and dedicated people are working frantically to avert the coming disasters. Nonetheless, those in power go about as if there is nothing wrong, playing out the final catastrophe of the Judeo-Christian ethic of Earth ownership by humankind proclaimed in the Book of Genesis.

John: I have a few questions.

Chasing Deer: Please, go ahead.

John: When Sweet Medicine says that newcomers will "quickly move from one place to another," do you think that he was foreseeing our present lifestyle, or did he mean something else?

Chasing Deer: That is a perceptive question, Grandson. It is really a very important criticism of American culture, but one that may not be easily seen by a non-native. You see, to us, the Creator put us in different places and gave us the responsibility to care for that place, to honor it, and to protect it. These places in turn taught us both about the Creator and ourselves. Thus, an Apache or an Abenaki would feel out of place here in the Great Plains, as I would in either the desert or the deep, eastern forest. After all, how can you learn to care for a place or learn its mysteries and its lessons if you do not stay there?

This land where we sit is alive for me. It holds a lifetime of memories and relationships, and I have many friends here: Some are streams, some are rocks, and some are trees. And I have animal friends. Have you not seen the fox that comes by nearly every day? I have known that fox family for more than 100 years. I can show you where I first kissed my wife. I can show you where Sitting Bull prayed. I can show you where the great seven-foot-tall Lakota warrior Touch the Clouds wept for his People and for his friend Crazy Horse when they killed him. I could go on forever, Grandson. The very ground upon which you sit is the dust of my ancestors, which is why I sit down gently and say *"Mitakuye Oyasin"* [all my relations].

Sitting Bull said that the white man would never understand the Indian. I don't know, John—but it seems to me that more and more of your youth are coming to us to seek that which they know, deep in their hearts, that their culture has deprived them of.

Perhaps if I read you some things from Indians born even before I was you may get an idea of the sacredness in which each tribe held its land. For example, around 1900, the United States government was trying to get the San Luis

Rey Indians to surrender more of their land. This is what Cecilo Blacktooth told them:

> You ask us to think what place we like best to this, where we have always lived. You see the graveyard out there? There are our fathers and grandfathers. You see that eagle-nest mountain and that rabbit-hole mountain? When God made them, He gave us this place. We have always been here. We do not care for any other place. . . . We have always lived here. We would rather die here. Our fathers did, and we cannot leave them.
>
> Our children were born here—how can we go away? If you give us the best place in the world, it is not so good for us as this. . . . This is our home. . . . We cannot live anywhere else. . . . We want this place and not any other.
>
> There is no other place for us. We do want you to buy any other place. If you will not buy this place, we will go to the mountain like quail, and die there—the old people and the women and children. Let the government be glad and proud. It can kill us. We do not fight. We do what it says. If we cannot live here, we want to go to the mountain and die. We do not want any other home.

John: I see what you mean. What an intense love—it's almost as if it were a person that she was talking about.

Chasing Deer: It is—it is her Mother. Grandson, I could read you hundreds of accounts that are just as intense or even more so, but I will read you just one more. It was written by an observer as President Jackson was removing the Choctaw from their homelands against their will. I can never read this one without a deep sadness welling up in my heart because it shows such a love of the Earth. The observer wrote " . . . the women made a formal procession through the trees surrounding their abandoned cabins, stroking the leaves of the oak and the elm trees in silent farewell." Many of us still have that type of connection to their tribal lands—after all, a man who is always on the move will never have a home, and there is no more precious gift than homecoming.

John: I think that I have a good idea of how the Indians must feel about their land. If we were to lose our farm in Virginia it would break my heart—my best memories of childhood are connected to the farm, and I know every inch of it.

Chasing Deer: That is good. Go there often, as it will renew your spirit and your heart to lie upon that ground. Are there any other questions?

John: Yes. I suppose that the sandlike food Sweet Medicine warned about is sugar and the strange drink is alcohol.

Chasing Deer: That's right.

John: It's my understanding that both alcoholism and diabetes are rampant on reservations, so Sweet Medicine was right when he warned the People not to eat or drink anything that the newcomers give them.

Chasing Deer: Sadly, what you say is true. If only the People had listened—but it is hard to hear even the most profound wisdom when you are taken from your land, sent to boarding school, and forbidden to speak your language or practice your religion. If it were not for the few strong ones among us, I imagine all would have been lost, just as what happened with the many extinct tribes.

John: Obviously liquor did not come to the Indian until whites came, but surely diabetes was present, wasn't it?

Chasing Deer: To the best of my knowledge, the first case of diabetes among Indians was not recorded until 1935, but as you said, Grandson, it is rampant now. As is heart disease, which was so rare when I was child. In fact, on some reservations, male life expectancy has dropped as much as 40 years. And this all started when our natural way of life was put to an end by the American government and we were forced on to reservations.

John: Certainly the government saw to it that the Indians were well fed on the reservations, right?

Chasing Deer: If they had, maybe things would not be so bad now. No, we were given starch, sugar, and meat that had as much as a 40-percent fat content. I do not think that you understand the attitude of the United States government toward us, Grandson. In 1872, the Commissioner of Indian Affairs, Francis Walker, said, "There is no question of national dignity . . . involved in the treatment of savages by a civilized power." And later he added that the government could reduce "the wild beasts to the condition of the supplicants of charity." Things have changed little, I am afraid.

John: That's terrible. I think I have a little understanding now of the legacy that's allowed the slaughter of native peoples in such countries as El Salvador, Guatemala, Honduras, and Brazil to take place.

Chasing Deer: Yes, sadly, it continues.

John: So are you telling me that if I went to a reservation today, I wouldn't find the same noble, healthy, and vibrant people that you've been telling me about?

Chasing Deer: No, Grandson, you would not. We are growing stronger and our spirit is returning, but we have so far to go. As my late friend Chief Luther Standing Bear wrote in the 1930s:

> Today you see but a shattered specimen, a caricature, if you please, of a man that once was. . . . Today my people, and all native people of this continent, are changed— degraded by oppression and poverty into but a semblance of their former being; health is undermined by disease, and

the moral and spiritual life of the people deaden by the loss of the great sustaining forces of the devotional ceremonies.

John: Why couldn't the People continue with their spiritual ceremonies? Surely that would have helped them in a time of such calamity.

Chasing Deer: They were outlawed, Grandson, in violation of the Bill of Rights.

John: Oh, I'm sorry, Grandfather. I had no idea. . . . I don't have any other questions about the prophecy at the moment. I need to be alone to think. My world is not what I thought it was.

CHAPTER THREE

White Buffalo Calf Maiden

Even though the moon was high in the night sky and most people would have been thinking about sleep by now, Chasing Deer merely stoked the fire and waited for John to return.

John: All right, Grandfather. I think I've processed that last story, and I'm ready for another one.

Chasing Deer: Good, Grandson. I hoped you would say that, because I want to tell you about an important cultural hero of my father's people—who, believe it or not, was a woman.

The Story of White Buffalo Calf Maiden

Long, long ago, the seven nations of the Lakota were camped together in midsummer for ceremonial and social activities. It was a very hot summer and food was scarce. Chief Standing Hollow Horn sent two brave warriors out from the camp to search for game that the People might eat. The two young warriors left on foot, for this was long before the Lakota had horses. No matter where they looked, they could not find any game. They decided to climb a hill from where they could see far over the plains. In the distance, they noticed a figure walking toward them. As it got closer, they knew that it must be a sacred being of some sort, for it floated more than it walked.

As the figure came closer, the two men could see that it was a young woman. In front of her, she carried both a bundle and a fan of sage. She was beautiful and radiant, and dressed in colors so magnificent and clear that they could not have been of this Earth. Her exquisite dress had sacred markings and quillwork such as the boys had never seen before. The sparkle and shine in her eyes told of a woman with great power. In fact, the young woman who approached them was White Buffalo Calf Maiden—a holy woman of *unequaled* power.

She was more beautiful than any woman that either of the young men had ever seen or imagined. Unfortunately, one of the boys began to have less-than-pure thoughts about her, and as he approached, he stuck out his hand to touch her. Instantly, he was struck down by lightning—and all that remained was a pile of burned bones. (Others say that a large cloud enveloped him and when it dissipated, one could see many snakes that had left not a bit of flesh upon him. His lust and forwardness with a sacred woman had eaten him up.)

White Buffalo Calf Maiden called the other young man to her side and instructed him to go back to his village and report everything that he had seen. He was also to tell the People that she was from the Buffalo Nation and had messages for them. He did what he was told, and informed the chief of all that had passed.

The chief listened to the young man with great respect, and told the entire village to prepare for the arrival of a Spirit Being. And so, the largest and most sacred of the medicine tipis was raised and prepared. The People waited, and after four days, they saw the holy maiden approaching the village carrying a large bundle. When she arrived, the chief escorted her to the medicine lodge, which she entered and circled in the direction of the sun.

Next, she prepared an altar with a buffalo skull and taught the people a number of sacred rituals and how to perform them in a good way. When that was done, she took from her bundle the Sacred Pipe, the *Chanupa Wakan,* the greatest spiritual gift that our People have received. She held the bowl in her left hand and the stem in her right. (This is still how pipes are held as they are getting ready to be smoked today.) Chief Standing Hollow Horn dipped some sweetgrass into a bag of water and gave it to the holy maiden, telling her that they had no food to offer her and to please forgive them. (Even today, when a person is to be purified before a ceremony, sweetgrass is dipped in water and sprinkled over them.)

White Buffalo Calf Maiden then taught the People how to use the Sacred Pipe. She filled the bowl with the inside bark of a red willow, and then she walked around the lodge in the way of the sun circling the Earth. This represented the Great Sacred Hoop of Life—the circle without beginning or end. White Buffalo Calf Maiden reached into the fire and lit the pipe with a hot coal, and the fire that emerged was the flame that was to be passed from generation to generation. She taught the People that the smoke that arose from the pipe was sacred. It was the very living Breath of the Great Mysterious One, whom we call Grandfather. This sacred breath of smoke would carry the People's prayers to the Above Beings.

She taught the Lakota how to pray and how to approach the Sacred Ones. Then she taught them the pipe-filling song, which is still sung today when one fills one's pipe. She taught the People to raise the pipe to Grandfather in the sky above, and downward to our Grandmother Earth, and then to the Four Directions, thus recognizing the entire universe.

"With this holy pipe," she said, "you will walk like a living prayer. With your feet resting upon the Earth and the pipe stem reaching to the sky, you body forms a living bridge between the Sacred Beneath and the Sacred Above. The *Wakan Tanka* [Great Spirit] smiles upon us, because we are now as one: Earth, sky, all living things—the two-leggeds, the four-leggeds, the winged ones, the trees, the grasses. Together with the People, they are all related, one family."

She taught the People that it is the Sacred Pipe that holds all together, and that the buffalo carving on its red stone bowl stands for the blood and flesh of the People and for the Buffalo Nation. It is the buffalo that represents all of creation because he stands upon four legs, which represent both the four directions and the four ages of creation. The stem of the pipe stands for all the living things upon the breast of Grandmother Earth. Hanging from where the stem and bowl are connected are the feathers of the spotted eagle— the messenger of the Grandfather and the wisest of all that flies. In the pipe, all that is is joined together in its connect-edness—so when you hold your pipe in a sacred way, you are connected to all that is.

From her bundle, White Buffalo Calf Maiden also took out a small round stone and placed it upon the ground. "Upon this stone that I have laid before you," she said, "you will see engraved the seven circles that stand for the seven sacred ceremonies that I shall give to you. The seven circles also stand for the seven Lakota nations—in the pipe, you are all joined."

Next the holy maiden talked to the women of the village so that they might remember their great importance and role in the life of the tribe, for women were its sustainers. She took many things to show her sisters from her sacred womb bag, such as pemmican, turnips, and corn. And she showed them how to cook meat and vegetables by putting heated stones in water. Then she told them to always remember that they were as great as warriors, for without them, the tribe would cease to be. "This Sacred Pipe also binds men and women together in love," White Buffalo Calf Maiden continued. "In it, both the men and the women share in its making. The men shall make the bowls and the stems, and the women shall bead the pipe with the quills of the porcupine. When a man takes a wife, they shall both hold the pipe and their hands shall be bound together with red cloth, tying their lives together."

The holy maiden also talked to the children, reminding them that they were the future of the tribe and thus must prepare themselves in a good and sacred way. She told them that when they were grown, they too would smoke the Sacred Pipe, so they must prepare themselves by walking the good red road.

Then she addressed the tribe as a whole, saying that they were a pure and good People and for that reason, the Sacred Pipe was entrusted to them. However, this trust was not for them alone, but for all the People. "The Sacred Pipe is a living thing," she said. "The stone is red to ever remind you to lead a red life and to stay upon the good red road. I shall only tell you of one ceremony now—the others will be revealed to you over time. The first ceremony in which you are to use your pipes is one to keep the soul of a dead person, for through the soul of the dead you can talk to the Great Mysterious. When a person dies, it is a sacred day—and when his soul is released from this Earth, it is also a sacred day. On such an occasion, four women among the tribe will become sacred. It is these four women who will cut down the cottonwood tree for the sun dance."

White Buffalo Calf Maiden then told Chief Standing Hollow Horn: "My chief, never forget that this pipe is very sacred. It will carry you where you need to go. I am the four ages of creation. They all reside in me. In each generation that succeeds you, I shall return." And she turned to the People and said, "I shall see you again."

The holy maiden took leave of the Lakota, promising that she would return in the future should there be times of great need. As she walked away toward the West, she rolled over four times. After the first roll, she turned into a black buffalo; after the second, a brown buffalo; after the third roll, a red buffalo; and finally, after the fourth, she turned into a white buffalo calf. At this point, she walked into the horizon and could be seen no more.

White Buffalo Calf Maiden promised us seven sacred rituals: the one she gave to the People when she came and six others that would come through visions given to our medicine people. For many, many centuries, we have had our seven sacred rituals as promised. I will now briefly describe the seven ceremonies that have come to us from our holy maiden and cultural heroine.

John: Grandfather, before you begin to speak of the seven rituals, I have some questions about the story that I'd like to ask you.

Chasing Deer: Please, go ahead.

John: Are there any symbolic meanings in this story like there are in many of the religious stories that I'm familiar with from my own culture?

Chasing Deer: That is a good question, John. I should have pointed them out. According to Black Elk, the snakes that devour the lustful young warrior are not just a description of what happened to him, they also remind us that anyone who lives purely in the world of the senses and is attached to that world is doomed to be devoured by his own passion. Thus, the snakes represent our appetites when they are not guided by something higher—they will devour us.

John: So, the religion that White Buffalo Calf Maiden brought to the Lakota is not unlike Christianity, in the sense that our natural appetites will bring our downfall if they're not guided by spiritual principles. Is that right?

Chasing Deer: You have got the right idea, but there are differences. Our people are not, in the phrase of your generation, "uptight." We are incredibly respectful of things such as sexual matters, but talking about them and joking about them in a nonpersonal way is quite acceptable. We also do not have such a stringent concept of sin, and we certainly have no concept of Original Sin, as does Christianity. We see nothing dirty, so to speak, about any part of our humanness.

John: I noticed that in your grandson, Tommy, when he was my roommate in college. This nonattachment to physical things reminds me very much of the Buddhist concept by that name. Is that fair?

Chasing Deer: I really do not know much about Buddhism, but what little I know leads me to believe that our beliefs are similar in this respect. Wait a minute—let me get something from the house.

John: What have you got there, Grandfather?

Chasing Deer: I have two books from the 18th century. One is by the Jesuit priest Lafitau, who was a missionary to the Iroquois between 1712 and 1717. His *Customs of the American Indian* is considered a masterpiece in describing Indian life as it was back then. The other one is *Travels* by Jonathan Carver, who traveled among the Plains Indians from 1766 to 1767. It is a bit controversial in that Carver may have borrowed heavily from others, which, of course, does not detract from its accuracy. Anyway, you tell me if what I am going to read you sounds very Buddhist, not so much in doctrine as in behavior.

Lafitau writes:

> They are high-minded and proud, possess a courage equal to every trial; an intrepid valor; the most heroic constancy under torments; and an equanimity which neither misfortunes nor reverses can shake. . . . They never permit themselves to indulge in passion, but always from

a sense of honor and greatness of soul, appear masters of themselves.

` And Carver writes:

> An Indian meets death, when it approaches him in his hut, with the same resolution he has often faced in the field. His indifference relative to this important article, which is the source of so many apprehensions to most every other nation, is truly admirable. When his fate is pronounced by the physician, and it remains no longer uncertain, he harangues those about him with the greatest composure.

I would point out that the word *harangue* here is used in its primary meaning of a speech to an assembly of people, not an angry, loud speech, which is a secondary meaning.

These writings seem to me to be consistent with the life of a Buddhist monk. What do you think?

John: I think so, too. Both the Buddhist monk and the Indian have achieved a nonattachment to the physical, although from what I understand, the Indian reveled in his physicality and enjoyed his senses to the utmost. The Buddhist monk, on the other hand, is generally far more removed from the world of the physical. I can't imagine a celibate Indian!

I do find one difference, though: In the quote you read from Lafitau, I think that if one were describing a Buddhist monk, one would use the word *humble* rather than *proud*.

Chasing Deer: I certainly do think that *humble* would be a more apt word for a Buddhist monk. The idea that Lafitau was trying to get across here would have been better rendered by the word *self-assured,* rather than *proud.* Pride conjures up arrogance, which I can tell you from having read the book that it is not what he meant.

John: The composure before death that Carver notes reminds me of the Buddhist monk who set himself on fire to protest the Vietnam war. He didn't move an inch or say a word—he just sat there quietly until he fell over dead. I'll never forget that image.

Chasing Deer: The same was true for our People, with one exception. If an Indian were burned at the stake, which did occur, he would not issue any sign of either pain or fear; instead, he would sing of the bravery of his People and harangue, in the second sense of the word, his enemies.

John: Where do individuals get such strength, Grandfather?

Chasing Deer: I cannot speak for Buddhists, but for our People, it came from training that began in early childhood. There is something else, but I truthfully do not know in how many tribes it existed. I am speaking of meditation. And, again, we have this in common with Buddhists, although it was certainly not as pervasive.

John: The Indians meditated?

Chasing Deer: As I said, I do not know how many tribes did. The Cherokees' six-holed flutes were used for meditation, according to the Cherokee medicine man Hawk Little-john, who was a seventh-generation flutemaker. I also have a description from an Army physician in Arizona of a young Apache woman meditating. I'll tell you what happened. It's an interesting and true story.

During the Apache wars in the 1880s, there was a skirmish between a small group of Apaches and the United States Army. The Apaches were nestled in behind boulders, and the soldiers were down below. When the Apaches decided to retreat, some of the soldiers went to an area that the Apaches had been. There they found a young woman warrior who had had her knee shattered by an enemy bullet.

The soldiers carried her back to the fort's hospital, where the surgeon determined that the woman's leg had to be amputated above the knee. The painkiller that was used back then was laudanum, a tincture of opium. It was a precious commodity in the Far West, and the surgeon decided that he was not going to waste it on an enemy. The leg was to be amputated without anesthesia or anesthetic. In his notes, the surgeon describes how the young Apache closed her eyes and went into a trancelike state. The entire operation was performed without her either moving or giving any sign of pain.

John: That's pretty incredible. You would have had to master meditation to a profound degree to be able to do that!

Chasing Deer: I am afraid that I don't know enough about the practice, but something quite unusual was going on. Do you have any more questions about the coming of White Buffalo Calf Maiden?

John: Yes, Grandfather, I have three. I started out by asking you about symbolic meanings in the story—I'd like to know if the buffalo symbolizes anything, as well as what the red road and the four ages mean.

Chasing Deer: None of the three things that you mentioned are explained in the story of White Buffalo Calf Maiden—you would have to know something about our culture, our spirituality, and our mythology to know what was being talked about, so it is good that you asked.

The buffalo was at the heart of Lakota life, supplying our food, our housing, much of our clothing, and many of our tools. Its horns were used as cups, its sinew for sewing and fastening things together, and its bladder as a holding bag for water. There was little that we needed in the material world that this wonderful creature did not supply. So, given the immense importance it had in our lives, it naturally evolved into a symbol for the entire universe. When we see the buffalo, we see all of creation, especially the Earth and all that is upon Her. In fact, each part of the buffalo represents some aspect of creation. But there is more that she represents, which leads us to your next question.

The buffalo's four legs are a representation of the four ages that White Buffalo Calf Maiden mentioned. The number four plays a central role in much of our Lakota thought, which, I imagine, began with the Four Directions. According to our mythology, the world moves in a cycle, as does a human life, from birth to death. At the beginning of each cycle, the buffalo is in the West, holding back the waters that will come to end the cycle. With every year that passes from the beginning of a cycle, the buffalo loses one hair—and at the end of each cycle, it loses a leg. The four ages are called the Rock Age, the Bow Age, the Fire Age, and the Pipe Age, and they are essentially a movement from physicality to spirituality. It is my understanding that at the end of the cycle, the waters come and the cycle begins again.

John: This myth is very similar to one I've read in the Hindu tradition. According to this myth, the sacred or divine law, which is called the *Bull Dharma,* also has four ages. The four legs of the bull represent the ages of the total cycle. There is a difference, though: For the Hindu, the cycle begins in a state of pure spirituality; as the ages pass, this is lost or, rather, its light fades with time. The cycle ends with some catastrophic event, and then the phase of pure or original spirituality is restored and the entire cycle begins again.

The Hindus believe that the bull is now standing on his last leg. Is this also true for the Lakota?

Chasing Deer: It certainly is. What an amazing coincidence of myths!

John: I'm quite sure that similar myths are found in other traditions as well. I shall have to think about that. But what about the red road, Grandfather?

Chasing Deer: Ah, yes, the good red road. This is also related to the Four Directions. The red road runs from north to south—north here represents purity, while south represents the very source of life itself. So, it is a good, spiritually infused road. Now the black or the blue road, as it is sometimes called, is a very different one. It is destructive, for as it runs from east to west, it goes from light to darkness. Black Elk said of one who walks this road that he is "one who is distracted, who is ruled by his senses, and who lives for himself rather than for his people."

From the time of birth onward, the Lakota child is taught to live for the People. A person who does not live in such a way has no respect in the tribe and is considered a fool. Tomorrow night I will tell you tales of such a person, the Spider-Man Iktomi. Do you have any more questions?

John: Not at the moment, but I would like to know what the seven rites were and something about each of them.

Chasing Deer: That is just what I was going to tell you next. If I were to fully explain the complete meaning of any of these rites, we would be still be here when Grandfather Sun greeted us in the morning, so I will just give you the essentials. If you want to study them in detail, I suggest that you read *The Sacred Pipe* by Joseph Epes Brown. There you will find Black Elk's account of the rites as given to Mr. Brown.

I should also mention that the *Inipi* and the *Hanblecheya* were ceremonies that we had before White Buffalo Calf Maiden came. What she added was the use of the pipe in these ceremonies.

Let us begin.

1. The *Inipi* (Sweat Lodge)

The *Inipi* is a rite of purification. It is used both as a rite in and of itself, as well as before any religious ritual and before embarking on any important task. Today it is commonly called a sweat lodge.

The lodge itself represents the entire universe. The water that is used is representative of the Thunder Beings, who, even though they are frightening, bring good things to our lives. The rocks represent the Earth and The Great Mysterious, for they are seen as eternal and cannot be destroyed. The willow branches, from which the frame of the lodge is made, remind us that all things blossom and die, but that death is only a transition to the Spirit World. These branches, of which there are usually 16, are set in such a way as to be symbolic of the Four Directions, making the center of the lodge both the center of the Earth and the center of the universe. The fire is the power of Spirit. The door is always facing the East, from which comes the light, which itself is representative of wisdom. Lastly, the earth that has been taken from the center of the lodge to make the rock pit is used to make an altar in front of the lodge.

The red-hot stones are placed in a hole in the center of the lodge and water is thrown upon them, thus producing a very hot steam that causes intense perspiration. We believe that impurities in the body are brought out in the sweat: The combination of Earth's two oldest elements—the *Inyan Wakan,* or sacred stones, and the *Mini Wakan,* or sacred water—releases the water Spirits to cleanse us. It is not only a physical cleansing, but a spiritual and emotional one as well. In the great discomfort and weakening of the body, the ego, as your people call it, drops away and the heart comes forth. It is only through the heart that we connect with the Above Beings and all our relations here on Grandmother Earth.

There is no place for pretense or vainglory in an *Inipi.* One's heart must speak the truth—the truth of our joys, our sorrows, our hopes and dreams, our successes and failures, our fear, and our pain. To be in an *Inipi* and hold back anything that is in one's heart is a form of dishonesty before *Tunkashila,* our Grandfather, and our Earthly relatives sweating with us. This is why many of your men, John, are uncomfortable in our lodges. They find it frightening and unmanly to reveal themselves to others, so they prefer to live in images and facades. This is why Fools Crow called the white man a mutant. For your people, it is unmanly to cry, but for our people, it is unmanly *not* to cry. Thus, your people so often remain in denial of the deepest, best part of themselves. That is no way to live.

One has only to look at your homeless, your poor, your uncalled-for wars, your destruction of the Earth, your blatant materialism and greed, and your self-centered leaders with hearts of stone to see what your "manliness" has produced. A fully developed man, as we see it, is comfortable expressing *all* of his emotions. How can one be truly grateful or joyous without tears? Our tears show our deep connection to something so they are appropriate whenever that connection is felt—be it in sorrow, joy, love, guilt, or anger.

Since all that is said and prayed about in the lodge goes into the tobacco and is released to the Sacred One as the pipe is smoked, one must be sure to have only spoken the truth of one's heart, for our Grandfather has no time to hear lies or half-truths. And, how can one's Earthly relatives be of help if they do not know the truth of your life? For part of the function of an *Inipi* is that by your honest revelations and prayers, others are able to help you. However, if your prayers are not fully the truth, then you deny your relatives the greatest gift that one human being can give to another—the opportunity to be of service.

John: What you have said, Grandfather, reminds me of Kierkegaard.

Chasing Deer: I am afraid that I do not know who that is. Can you explain?

John: Søren Kierkegaard is, to me at least, the most profound of all the Christian philosophers. What I'm reminded of here is his belief that it was the task of every person to become revealed.

Chasing Deer: Precisely! At the heart of all spiritual traditions, one tends to find the same things, for we all bleed red. By that, I mean we are all human. Please do not let me ever give you the impression that our Indian way is the only way, or the best way. It is simply *our* way. When you find me critical of your culture it is because the world needs a wake-up call, as I believe is the expression used these days. There are things that both cultures can contribute to the welfare of all, not just the privileged few.

As humans are by nature tribal animals, it seems essential to me that if the human world is to be saved and served, so to speak, then it had better go look at its roots. Prophecies from many of our nations have been warning us for some time that we are at a turning point of great consequence. Either we regain our spiritual footing or we are doomed to more poverty, more war, and the further destruction of the Earth—destruction to the point where She can no longer support us and, like a cancer, we will be excised. We have become like an ungrateful child who is poisoning the very breast that feeds him. If I seem harsh, do not take it as personal, racial, or cultural—but there looms a great fear and a deep sorrow for all people inside of me.

Your people are caught in ways that we never were, and I feel compassion for them. Let me give you an example: When we were living tribally, no man had to go to war if he chose not to. It was the individual's decision. There was no president or king to tell him that he must—chiefs had no such power. This was why in the wars against my People we often turned dead soldiers facedown to the ground. As we saw it, no man who took orders from another to kill deserved to look upon the heavens. To this day, it is most unseemly for an Indian to tell another Indian what to do.

Your people have to pay taxes to pay for wars, most of which are uncalled for and imperialistic. If you do not pay, you go to jail. Your moral autonomy is compromised in a way that we would never have allowed. If we had taxes in the old days, there was nothing anyone could do if a person decided to pay only the percentage for what he thought were good social purposes.

John: But what about those who wouldn't pay taxes simply because they wanted the money for themselves?

Chasing Deer: That way of thinking would have been so foreign to us as to never come up. One was trained from birth to live one's life for the good of the tribe.

Here, let me read you something from Tom Newcombe, who lived with us during the time of Crazy Horse. He was a scout for our nemesis, General Miles. Newcombe told Ernest Thompson Seton, author of *The Gospel of the Redman:*

> I tell you, I never saw more kindness or Christianity anywhere. The poor, the sick, the aged, the widows, and the orphans were always looked after first. Whenever we moved camp, someone took care that the widows' lodges were moved first and set up first. After every hunt, a good-size chunk of meat was dropped at each door where it was most needed. I was treated like a brother; and I tell you I have never seen any community of church people that was as truly Christian as that band of Indians.

Remember, Grandson, that this was at a time when we were constantly under attack by the United States. And our People were not the only ones who noticed this. The first-known Euro-American to come into contact with both the Nez Perce and the Flatheads was Captain Bonneville, after whom the Bonneville Salt Flats was named. He wrote:

> Simply to call these people religious would convey but a faint idea of the deep hue of piety and devotion which pervades their whole conduct. Their honesty is immaculate, and their purity of purpose and their observance of the rites of their religion are most uniform and remarkable. They are certainly more like a nation of saints than a horde of savages.

Grandson, my point is this: If my People could live like this before the invasion, then why can we all not learn to live like this? If you want to make good buffalo stew, then it is wise to seek out those who have made it before!

Now I think that it is time to move on to the next rite or I am going to be mighty tired tomorrow morning when I get up to pray at sunrise.

John: I could listen to you all night, Grandfather.

Chasing Deer: And I could probably talk all night! But it is time to move on.

2. The *Wiwanyag Wachipi* (Sun Dance)

The *Wiwanyag Wachipi*, or sun dance, which is held every summer, was given to the People through a vision. In its essence, it is a ceremony of thanksgiving and renewal. It is never done for oneself or to show one's bravery and stamina—it is a gift to the Grandfathers for hearing our prayers or for renewing the Earth, or as a supplication for another or the People as a whole. Indeed, seldom are our ceremonies done for ourselves, but for the People. Often you will hear the following prayer prior to many ceremonies: *"Tunkashila, onshimala ye oyate wani wachin cha"* or "Grandfather, have pity on me that my People may live."

We give of our flesh because to the Lakota, our bodies are the only thing that we truly own. Unlike a material gift, it shows that we are serious and committed in our supplications and are willing to suffer for them.

Traditionally, a cottonwood tree is used for the sun-dance pole. It is selected and cut in a ritual all its own, and special prayers with the Sacred Pipe are used. The same holds true as it is erected and put into place. Long leather strips are tied to the pole. At the end of the leather strip, there will be a strong bone or twig that is inserted under the skin of the sun dancer once he has been pierced on both sides of the chest.

The dancer will dance to the rhythm of the drums and the sun-dance songs until he has broken free from the tree. This usually takes many hours and is quite strenuous, as the dancer has been fasting from both food and water and has sweated in the lodge prior to the dance.

Each dancer has filled his or her pipe in a sacred way, and it has been placed on the Sun Dance Altar prior to the dancing commencing. Traditionally, if a dancer needs to rest, then his pipe is given to the singers. If the singers accept the pipe, then the dancer may rest while the singers smoke the pipe. Should the number of pipes upon the altar be more than the number of rests taken, then the dancers must smoke the remaining pipes in the sacred lodge when they are done.

The sun dance is presided over by a medicine man, whose chief duties are to use his pipe to bless the Sun Dance Tree, to bless the space in which the dance is held, to lead the sweat lodges, and to greet the rising sun each morning of the ceremony.

As times have changed, there are variations in the ceremony today. Nonetheless, the dedication of the dancers, and the dance's sacred meaning and intent has not changed over these many centuries that the People have danced.

3. The *Hanblecheya* (Vision Quest)

In the *Hanblecheya*, or the vision quest as it is often referred to, one seeks by prayer and fasting to be given a vision by the Spirits. For many, it is seen as a necessary ceremony in attaining both one's identity and maturity. Often the entire course of a man's life would be determined by his visions.

Traditionally, one would consult with a medicine man prior to seeking a vision. This process of preparing could take a year or more, although there was no set amount of time for one's preparation to cry for a vision. As with our other ceremonies, the vision quest was not so much for one's self as it was for the People. It was an attempt to learn in what way or capacity one could best serve.

In preparation for the *Hanblecheya,* the person made 500 tobacco ties that would serve to delineate his or her sacred space, which was covered with sage upon which the person sat. The only objects inside of the sacred space were the person's Sacred Pipe, a wooden bowl, and a robe for warmth. At each of the four corners of the sacred space were placed the colored flags of the Four Directions.

Prior to going up to the isolated mountain or hill (usually Bear Butte, our Sacred Mountain in South Dakota) the seeker had an *Inipi* ceremony to purify himself. The seeker would stay upon the mountain for four days and nights without food or water as prayers were offered to the Four Directions. The prayers were almost continuous, while the seeker held his pipe extended toward the direction in which he was praying and calling for a vision to come to him. When his four days were up, the medicine man's assistant would bring him down for another *Inipi,* in which he would tell of his experience and it would be interpreted for him by the medicine man.

One never questions the visions of another—they are sacred to that person and will determine the path that he is to walk in his life. Lastly, the Spirits will hold a person accountable to the vision that they have given him.

One is as often as not unsuccessful in obtaining a vision the first time that one is sought. However, there is no limit to the number of times that one may choose to cry for a vision. Indeed, medicine men are often upon the mountain seeking visions, for that is how they get both their power and their instructions. And it was through the *Hanblecheya* that the sacred rites of the Lakota were given to them by White Buffalo Calf Maiden.

4. The *Nagi Gluha* Ceremony (Keeping of the Soul)

White Buffalo Calf Maiden gave the *Nagi Gluha,* or The Keeping of the Soul ceremony, to us when she first came to us long ago. The reason for the ceremony is so that the soul of the departed can be purified and can then join itself with *Wanka Tanka,* The Great Mysterious. One does not want one's soul wandering about the Earth as do the souls of those who have not lived well.

The ceremony requires the cutting of a lock of hair from a newly deceased person, which is then kept in a scared bundle that has been especially prepared to hold the hair for a year or more. During the Keeping of the Soul, the sacred bundle is never left alone, and a woman of high character should be its guardian—in fact, the first such woman to perform this sacred duty was Red Day Woman.

The keeper of the soul should live as flawlessly as possible while carrying out this duty; and the tribe, in turn, should feed the keeper and bring gifts. During the time of this keeping, the tribe and the family are expected to live as flawlessly as possible. When the year or so is up, a feast is given for all the People and all the gifts made for the honoring of the deceased person are given away to the poorest families. Afterwards, a Pipe Ceremony and a Release of the Soul ritual are held.

5. The *Hunkapi* Ceremony
(Making of Relatives)

The *Hunkapi* Ceremony, or the Making of Relatives, is held between two individuals, two groups, or even two nations (as was the first Making of Relatives ceremony, which was between the Arikara and the Lakota). In the ceremony, relationships are established that are even stronger than blood ties. If the ceremony is done between two individuals, then the two so bound are each other's *Hunka*. There is nothing that one would not do for one's *Hunka*, including sacrificing one's life or taking over the responsibilities for a *Hunka's* family should one's *Hunka* die. It was a lifelong commitment of the strongest sort.

6. The *Isna Ti Alowan* (The Buffalo Ceremony)

The *Isna Ti Alowan,* or The Buffalo Ceremony, is used to honor and to purify a girl when she reaches womanhood. At this time, the girl is proclaimed a "sacred woman" and told that she will bear sacred children. During the ceremony, she is given instructions on being a woman, reminded of how necessary it is to lead a life worthy of her tribe, and pledges to raise her children as Lakota.

7. The *Tapa Wanka Yeyapi* Ceremony (Tossing of the Ball)

The last of the Seven Ceremonies of the Lakota is the *Tapa Wanka Yeyapi,* or the Tossing of the Ball. In this ceremony, as many people can participate as who wish to. The participants position themselves at each of the four corners of the sacred hoop. A young woman, symbolic of White Buffalo Calf Maiden, stands in the center holding the ball made of buffalo hide and hair, which is symbolic of the entire universe. When all are in place in the four corners, she tosses the ball in accord with Lakota custom in the manner of the sun, going from west to north to east to south, and whoever catches the ball returns it to the center. When the ball has been tossed to all the four directions, it is then tossed again, but this time high into the air. Everyone is eligible to catch the ball, and whoever does so is thought to be the recipient of a great blessing in the future. After the ball is caught, all the participants smoke the Sacred Pipe and gifts are given to the one who caught the ball. The ceremony ends with a large feast for all.

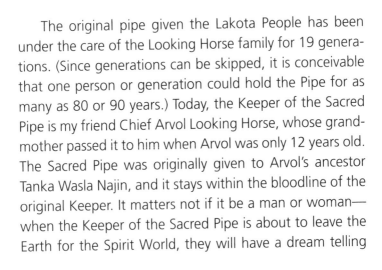

The original pipe given the Lakota People has been under the care of the Looking Horse family for 19 generations. (Since generations can be skipped, it is conceivable that one person or generation could hold the Pipe for as many as 80 or 90 years.) Today, the Keeper of the Sacred Pipe is my friend Chief Arvol Looking Horse, whose grandmother passed it to him when Arvol was only 12 years old. The Sacred Pipe was originally given to Arvol's ancestor Tanka Wasla Najin, and it stays within the bloodline of the original Keeper. It matters not if it be a man or woman— when the Keeper of the Sacred Pipe is about to leave the Earth for the Spirit World, they will have a dream telling them who the next Keeper should be.

White Buffalo Calf Woman told the people that she would return to them, and her return tells the Lakota People that their prayers are still being heard and that she is with them. Late in the summer of 1994, at the farm of Val and Dave Heider, a white buffalo calf (that was not an albino) was born—and the Heiders named her Miracle. On the day Miracle was born, the Oglala Lakota medicine man Floyd Hand had a vision of her birth. His vision also told him of the calf's father's death from an intestinal blockage that would occur shortly after the calf was born. Floyd Hand left Pine Ridge and traveled to the Heiders' farm in Janesville, Wisconsin, to tell them.

Miracle's father did, indeed, die as Floyd had said and an autopsy revealed the cause as an intestinal blockage. In an interview, this is what Floyd had to say:

> I started to tell others that White Buffalo Calf Woman is coming back—that the Virgin Mary is coming back when the cherries are black. I kept this up from 1988 to 1994. In March of 1994, about 65 people were praying together in Minnesota where I was leading a prayer session, when she appeared. She said that when the cherries are black, she would return and her father would take her place. Her father would die so that she could live. She would come back. She would give us these messages.

The prophetic messages that Floyd received from White Buffalo Calf Woman were the following:

First, the four races of humankind have not lived up to their responsibilities to the Earth. Because of this, women shall become more powerful to restore balance to the world and lead the nations of the world. This will begin in the East among Asian people.

Second, the evils of the world shall turn against each other and destroy themselves. During the years from 1997 to 1999 there will be a great famine as more and more of the Earth becomes desert. We will see governments in turmoil and many of the powerful will lose their positions and new governments shall be formed.

Third, the destruction of both the Earth and her peoples will accelerate. This will be brought about by both natural and manmade disasters. Wars, earthquakes, floods, and so forth will become more common as time goes by. White Buffalo Calf Woman said that in the 21st century the entire Earth shall be covered by a cloud for about 130 days. Finally, in the 21st century, in the 21st year and on the 21st day, harmony and love will return to the Earth through her guidance.

Lastly, new nations will arise as the old nations crumble and facilitate this new beginning for Earth and her peoples. White Buffalo Calf Woman will be of service to all nations and races.

It was this divine message, which was not new with Floyd, that became the basis for the Lakota saying that when White Buffalo Calf Women returned as a white buffalo that she would change her colors from white, to black, to yellow,[1] and, finally, to red. This Miracle has done. It is clear that most of the prophecies given to Floyd are unfolding, while others, like the great famines in Africa during the late 1990s have already come to pass. We shall see. Frankly, I am not so hopeful.

Shortly before Miracle was born, two eagles flew down and circled Dave Heider on his farm. So far, [as of 1997] 23 eagles have arrived at Miracle's birthplace. To us they represent the Spirits telling us that bad times are coming and that we had better wake up soon.

It must be said that the Heiders were so impressed and touched by the thousands of visitors that came to their farm and all the prayer ties and other gifts that were brought to honor Miracle that they have refused to sell her to the rich and famous who have tried to buy her. They have also refused to give the fence with all the sacred gifts hanging from it to the Smithsonian Institute when they offered to buy it.

I am glad to report that Miracle is alive and well and a mother herself. Two other white buffalo have joined her, and the Lakota await the birth of the fourth as their prophecies proclaimed.

And now, Grandson, I think it is time for me to stop speaking, or we will miss sleep altogether on this night!

---

[1]Earlier it was stated that the white buffalo would change from black to brown. The actual color, from the many that I have seen, is a very dirty yellow or a very light dusty brown. To anyone familiar with this shade of buffalo, it is clear that it could be called either yellow or brown.

PART II

The
Teaching
Tales of
Iktomi

CHAPTER FOUR

A Day in the Life of Foolish Iktomi

Chasing Deer: When will you be leaving, Grandson?

John: In two days, I'm afraid.

Chasing Deer: Well, then, I am going to spend our remaining evenings telling you some stories about Iktomi.

John: Is he another cultural hero?

Chasing Deer: Heavens no! He's our antihero, if you will. *Iktomi* is the Lakota word for "spider," so Iktomi is "the

Spider-Man." He is capable of changing himself into a spider and back into a man again.

John: What exactly do you mean by "antihero"?

Chasing Deer: Let me tell you something of the purpose of the tales that I am going to tell you and put them in a Lakota cultural context.

Contrary to many people's perception of us, you will scarcely find a group that laughs as much as we do. We just love funny stories—the more ribald, the better! Yet, despite the humorous nature of most of the Iktomi stories, they are often actually quite serious in nature. You see, Grandson, the stories of Iktomi are usually about our human foibles. One could think of them as showing us our frailties and weaknesses, and the unfortunate results that occur when we give in to them.

As a communal people in whom Spirit infuses every aspect of our life, these stories serve to reinforce the need to act honestly, generously, and in a good way. The Lakota were well aware that each individual was only as strong as the community that, as a mother, nourished them.

The stories of Iktomi always seem to be of a dual nature to me: While they are always humorous, the messages that they carry about human behavior are very serious to the People. Iktomi himself is a rather intriguing, amoral character. He is far from stupid, yet his ingenuousness gets him into one dilemma after another. His self-centeredness always foils his ingenuity and keeps him from getting what he wants.

Iktomi is a trickster . . . actually, he's more of a prankster—a character who runs through the stories of many tribes across the land. His tales are not unlike the stories found in many religions, except that they focus much more on what results when one ignores the principles of healthy relationships and communal life.

It is not altogether easy for a nontribal person to understand the full force and meaning of the Iktomi stories. One will often hear a Lakota say the phrase *"Mitakuye Oyasin,"* which means "all my relations." It is said in many contexts and is pervasive in its use among the Lakota. One will hear it used when a person enters the sweat lodge, when a person is finished praying, when the Sacred Pipe is passed, and when one gives another tobacco, to name a few. The "relations" here do not refer only to our fellow humans but to the entire natural world—indeed, this can refer to the entire universe, including those in the spirit world. The American Indian is well aware of the interconnectedness of everything. We believed that it was one of our sacred duties not to disrupt the natural harmony of things, since all of Grandmother Earth's children were on an equal footing, so to speak. We humans have no more rights than the buffalo, the stream, or the air. This is diametrically opposed to the view of the Western Christian world, where the Earth and all that is upon Her, and even *in* Her, are for humans to use and exploit as they see fit.

John: This is actually something that I know about, thanks to an ecology course I once took. The class structure you mention was seen in nature and taken directly from the Bible, and then it was transferred to society. In the late 19th century, the English philosopher and sociologist Herbert Spencer reinforced this idea by applying a perversion of Darwin's thought to social class and exploitation. Darwin very seldom used the term *evolution* or the phrase "survival of the fittest." Spencer popularized them both—and his use of "evolution" helped give racism a seemingly scientific basis. "Survival of the fittest" was used to justify the exploitation of the poor, the uneducated, and so forth by the rich and powerful, which, obviously, has no scientific basis.

Chasing Deer: Now *you* are teaching *me!* I like that.

John: Thank you, Grandfather. I had the feeling that you weren't through with your thoughts about man's relationship to the Earth. I know that it's horribly impolite in Indian society to ever interrupt, so I owe you an apology.

Chasing Deer: Think nothing of it; after all, you are not an Indian yet! Yes, I would like to say a bit more on this subject, as I think it is important for you to see that our way of thinking is still alive and well. In 1990, the Onondaga chief Oren Lyons was one of the representatives of the Native Peoples of the Americas at an international human-rights meeting. Later, Chief Lyons said, "We went to Geneva, the Six Nations (Iroquois), and the great Lakota Nation as representatives of the indigenous people of the Western Hemisphere, and what was the message that we gave? 'There is a hue and a cry for human rights,' they said, 'for all people.' And we (the indigenous people) said, 'What of the rights of the natural world? Where is the seat for the buffalo or the eagle? Who is representing them here in this forum? Who is speaking for the waters of the Earth? Who is speaking for the trees and the forests? Who is speaking for the fish, for the whales, for the beavers, for our children?'"

Now, Grandson, compare what Chief Lyons said to the following by the Christian theologian Harvey Cox of Harvard University in his book *The Secular City:* "Just after his creation, man is given the crucial responsibility of naming the animals. He is their master and commander. It is his task to subdue the earth." Quite a difference between the two, I would say.

John: Quite a *big* difference! Chief Lyons speaks of all the animals and so forth as equals to himself, whereas Mr. Cox puts them in a very subordinate position, not that of relatives as in *"Mitakuye Oyasin."*

Chasing Deer: Exactly! There is all the difference between a relative and a slave. Now I would like to move on to a few other things so that the meaning of the stories of Iktomi will be clearer to you.

The Lakota were strongly egalitarian, which does not mean that some did not have more than others—they did. But it was the tribe's and the chief's responsibility to see that all were cared for. After a buffalo hunt, the best meat was always left before the lodges of the aged and the widowed. A common saying was: "If one is hungry, then all shall be hungry."

The Lakota also eschewed competition among children, as they did physical punishment, for all were seen to have their gifts to offer the tribe. It was also unthinkable to in any way demean someone who was either handicapped or different in any way. For instance, those who were gay were allowed to live as they so chose, and usually, by about age 18, would decide to follow either a woman's or a man's path. In fact, one of the greatest warriors to fight with Crazy Horse was named Women Dress because he preferred to dress as a woman. One never questioned the individuality of another, for each person was given his or her role in the community—and as often as not, that person was following the visions he or she was given by the Spirits.

The great respect given to individuality can be illustrated by the life of Crazy Horse himself. In the tribe, he was often referred to as "Our Strange Man" because he seldom attended council meetings or ceremonies. He did not dress extravagantly as many did for war; instead, he dressed quite simply, which he was instructed to do in one of his visions. And he would often leave the tribe for extended periods to be alone, for he was a mystic.

Every so often the tribe would select four shirt wearers among the young men. This was the highest of honors, recognizing the very best of the young men. It became a shirt wearer's responsibility to be sure that all in the tribe were looked after—that is, to become aware of what needs there were in the tribe and to be sure that those needs were met. Even though Crazy Horse was known as "Our Strange Man," he was chosen as a shirt wearer. So you can see how much each person's path and individuality was respected.

John: That's very different from the world I live in. Anyone the slightest out of the ordinary wouldn't be named dogcatcher!

Chasing Deer: Yes, I have noticed that! You must remember that for the Lakota, concern for the welfare of the tribe as a whole was an overriding concern. It was not what your people would call a "commitment," it was life itself. A commitment, it seems to me, is an agreement and an act of will. This concern for the tribe went far deeper than that—it was the heart and soul of every Lakota. A people not raised in that way cannot really understand the depth of this feeling and concern.

Let me give you a most telling example from a tribe in South America. The great French writer Michel de Montaigne wrote the following in the 1570s:

> Three men of that nation, not knowing how dearly it will one day cost them in tranquility and happiness to know the corruptions of this side of the world, and that this intercourse will be the cause of their ruin (which indeed I imagine is already advanced—poor wretches, to be allured by the desire to see new things and to leave their own serene sky to come and see ours!) were at Rouen at a time when the late King Charles IX was there. The king had a long talk with them. They were shown our ways, our pomp,

the form of a fine city. Then somebody asked what they found most marvelous. They mentioned three things, the third of which I am sorry to have forgotten, but I still remember two. They said that in the first place they thought it quite strange that so many big men with beards, strong and armed, who were about the king (they were probably thinking of the Swiss who formed his guard) should submit to obey a child, rather than choosing one of their own number to command them. Second, they observed that some men among us were gorged full with all kinds of good things, while their halves (they have a way of speaking of men as if they were halves of one another) were begging at their doors, emaciated with hunger and poverty; they thought it strange that these necessary halves could suffer such injustice, and that they did not seize the others by the throat, or set to fire their houses.

John: That is amazing, Grandfather. I take it to mean that these Indians were so connected to each other that they could not even see themselves as complete or whole without their other tribal members. How different "halves" is from our "I" and "they." Now I can understand why in most tribes names were seldom used, but rather "brother," "sister," "father," "mother," and so forth. They literally did see each other as related, didn't they?

Chasing Deer: Yes, they did. Unfortunately, I truly think that unless you were raised tribally, you could never begin to feel as tribal people feel for one another. The poor Euro-American has to learn such things as "Do unto others as you would have others do unto you"—while for a tribal person, this is all he or she has ever known from birth.

Let me give you an actual example of this, which I recently witnessed on a reservation in Canada that has somehow been able to remain quite traditional in its ways. On three separate occasions, a child no older than six at the most was offered a piece of food (in one case, a cookie; and in the other two, a piece of fruit). In each case, the child who was handed the food sat down, and other children came and sat around him or her in a circle. The child who had been given the food then passed it to his or her left without taking a bite first, and the food was passed around and shared equally by all—none of the children attempted to take a giant bite. The food was thus passed along until it returned to the first child for the last bite. No adult had to tell these children to share their food—they simply knew to do it.

John: That's kind of hard to believe . . . not that I'm questioning you, Grandfather. In college I learned that that type of behavior in a young child was impossible. According to our developmental psychologists, children that young aren't yet what's called "fully socialized" and are basically very self-centered. What do you think accounts for such exceptional behavior? I've certainly never witnessed such a thing.

Chasing Deer: It really has to do with the way that we were brought up from birth. We learned by observing the example of those around us. Let me relate to you some things that the Lakota Chief Standing Bear and the Dakota

Ohiyesa or Charles Eastman, who were both born in the 19th century, wrote about their upbringing. Ohiyesa wrote:

> It has always been our belief that the love of possessions is a weakness to be overcome. Its appeal is to the material part, and if allowed its way it will in time disturb spiritual balance for which we all strive.
>
> Therefore, we must learn early the beauty of generosity. As children we are taught to give what we prize most, that we may taste the happiness of giving; at an early age we are made the family giver of alms. If a child is inclined to be grasping, or to cling too strongly to possessions, legends are related that tell of the contempt and disgrace falling on those who are ungenerous and mean.

And here is Chief Standing Bear relating his childhood learning:

> The Indians in their simplicity literally gave away all that they have—to relatives, to guests, or other tribes or clans, but above all to the poor and the aged, from whom they can hope for no return. . . .
>
> One lesson to learn was to be strong willed. Little children were taught to give and give generously. A sparing giver was no giver at all. Possessions were given away until the giver was poor in this world's goods and had nothing left but the delight and joy of pure strength. It was a bonded duty to give to the needy and the helpless. When mothers gave food to the weak and the old they gave portions to their children at the same time, so that the children could perform the service of giving with their own

hands. Little Lakota children often ran out and brought into the tipi an old and feeble person who chanced to be passing. If a child did this, the mother must at once prepare food. To ignore the child's courtesy would be unpardonable. But it is easy to touch the heart of pity in a child, so the Lakota was taught to give at any and all times for the sake of becoming strong and brave. The greatest brave was he who could part with his most cherished belongings and at the same time sing songs of joy and praise. It was a custom to hold "give-away dances" and to distribute presents that were costly and rare. To give is the delight of the Lakota.

So, you see, Grandson, sharing and generosity are all that we saw from the time we were born. While there are many things that separate our children from yours, I will cite only three more. By the time a Lakota child was six, he or she was able to sit alone in total silence for long periods of time. This taught the children to enjoy and feel all their senses and the world around them. Indeed, a child who could not do this was considered backward. The children were also trained very early on not to overeat, so there was no childhood obesity as is now rampant in America and, sadly, with our children as well, for too many of our people have taken to the ways of the dominant culture. Last, and this is important for understanding the stories of Iktomi, boasting or bragging was considered most unseemly. This is something our children also learned at a very early age.

If you will pardon me for seeming like I am bragging, it is simply the truth that most Lakota children by the time of puberty were more socially, morally, and spiritually aware than the vast majority of contemporary Euro-American adults.

And now, I think you are ready to hear the stories of Iktomi.

It was a bright, sun-filled day, and Iktomi had just gotten up. It was late in the day, of course, because Iktomi was very lazy. In fact, he probably would have stayed curled up in his buffalo robe for a great deal longer if his head had not itched so.

"Oh, these lice are dreadful!" he exclaimed.

As he wandered around scratching his head and trying to wake up he came across two beautiful maidens. They were hard at work tanning buffalo hides and discussing the various qualities of the many handsome and honorable young bachelors of the village.

Without being asked, Iktomi approached the young women and laid his head upon the lap of one of them. "Get rid of these lice for me—they are driving me crazy!" he demanded. This was not only impolite, but indeed, outrageous behavior, for a Lakota never demanded anything of another Lakota. Rather than express their outrage, the two maidens took turns combing Iktomi's tangled and dirty hair. So soothing was their gentle activity that Iktomi was soon quite drowsy and fell asleep.

When the young women heard Iktomi snoring, they knew for sure that he was sound asleep, so they stopped combing the interloper's hair. Instead, they began to fill his hair with burrs, those sticky, multipronged ones that seem almost impossible to remove. When Iktomi's hair was as full of burrs as a burr bush itself, the young women quietly left him.

Iktomi awoke to find the women gone and his head full of burrs. The skin on his face was drawn so tight that he could not even close his eyes! Since there was simply no other way to get rid of the burrs, Iktomi had to cut off all of his hair. Now a bald-headed Indian is a sight to see, and Iktomi brought roars of laughter upon himself wherever he went in the village. This was too much for our proud friend to bear, so he quietly and quickly left the village.

By noon that day, Iktomi was on his own, wandering wherever his feet took him. Before too long he came upon a beautiful, slow-flowing stream, which contained the most luscious and delicious-looking chokecherry trees and berry bushes. Of course, it did not even occur to the impulsive Iktomi, who always just wanted what he wanted, that these were the mere reflections of the trees and bushes above the stream. Into the water he jumped, gaining no berries but getting soaking wet!

All Iktomi could do now was lie in the bright sun and dry himself off. When he was dry, he continued his aimless journey and soon came upon an old funeral scaffold. Upon it lay an ancient warrior who had been dead for some time. Naturally a decaying body does not emit a pleasant odor, but one would never say so in the presence of the body for fear of offending the spirit of the person. No one, not even the dead, likes to be told that they smell! But that did not bother the impolite and self-centered Iktomi. "Ugh, this body stinks!" he cried.

The dead warrior could not help but hear this offending remark. He jumped down from his scaffold and grabbed Iktomi by the neck. "I heard what you said!" said the angry Spirit.

"Oh, you did," said Iktomi with a frightened smile. "Then why have you grabbed me by the neck? Do you not like being told that you smell of honey and fresh spring roses?"

To Iktomi's surprise, the Spirit let him go, and he ran away as fast as he could. Iktomi was so scared that he turned his two-leggedness into the eight-leggedness of his spider self, and he ran as he had never run before. (You can always tell when Iktomi is truly frightened, for he will use all eight of his legs in order to get away more rapidly.)

After he had put some distance between himself and the Spirit, Iktomi stopped to catch his breath and gather his wits. When his breath returned and his fear had subsided, Iktomi resumed his journey to nowhere in particular. He saw what looked like a pleasant path that seemed as though it wound around to a large cliff. As he approached, he saw an ancient medicine man sitting upon the ground praying.

"Oh, I am so hungry from fasting and praying," said the old man, and he began to sing a series of four songs.

"These are my buffalo songs," he explained to Iktomi, "and whenever I am hungry I sing them." No sooner had the medicine man finished the fourth song then a large, fat buffalo came rolling down the cliff toward them and stopped dead right at the medicine man's feet. "These are powerful songs," he continued. "I never have to worry about going hungry so long as I sing them in a good way with respect for the Buffalo Nation."

As one probably has already guessed by now, Iktomi wanted such powerful songs, so he begged, "Please, *please,* Grandfather, teach me the wonderful songs that you were singing!"

But the old medicine man was not so sure about Iktomi. His years of experience had taught him a lot about the character of men; for those who beg too hastily for what has power and is not theirs are often not to be trusted. The old sage was justly wary of this little man who was so eager to have his songs and he said so: "Whoever you are, I do not think that you deserve to have songs of such power. Something tells me that you are a foolish and very selfish person, certainly not one to be entrusted with such songs of power."

"Oh, but Grandfather, if it were me I surely would not even ask for your beautiful songs, but it is for my People. The buffalo have become scarce where we live. The People are starving, and I must help them. It is such a pitiful sight to see the tight bellies of the little children and the milk drying from the mothers' breasts."

The old medicine man took pity on Iktomi and his People, saying, "This is not good. Of course I shall give you the songs, and you must hurry back to the People and feed them. There is, however, one promise that you must make me before I teach you the songs. Never, ever use them unless the People can find nothing else to eat. Do you so promise?"

"Yes, Grandfather," Iktomi replied, "I can promise you that. I only want to be sure that my People never face starvation again."

So Iktomi stayed and learned the powerful buffalo songs from the medicine man. When the medicine man was satisfied that Iktomi knew the songs by heart, he sent him to feed his People. Iktomi thanked him and went on his way, humming his newly learned songs. As soon as Iktomi got far away from the old medicine man, he couldn't wait to try out his new songs. Iktomi sat down and sang the four songs just as he had learned them. No sooner had he finished than a large, plump buffalo rolled down the hill above him and fell dead at his feet. However, Iktomi was not the least bit hungry, so he took none of the precious meat. He simply left the dead buffalo there to rot, not even taking the large horns that would have made excellent cups for drinking. He had only sung the buffalo songs to amuse himself! Iktomi thought it was so funny that he had captured such power that he laughed all the way down the path as he continued his aimless wandering.

The very thought of the new power he commanded so excited Iktomi that he could not contain himself. Twice more he stopped to sing the magical songs that he had been taught by the compassionate medicine man, and twice more a buffalo rolled off a cliff dead at his feet. Of course, Iktomi had no intention of feeding anyone with his recently received power—his only intent was to both amuse himself and feel powerful.

However, one does not treat medicine gifts so lightly. To be given such a gift imposes a great responsibility on the recipient. If you want to anger the Spirits, you can do nothing more to offend them than to refuse to use their gifts with the same generosity as they were given. For a Lakota, to be lacking in generosity and honor is not to be a Lakota at all, so Iktomi should have known he was heading for trouble. Nonetheless, a fourth time he sang the magic buffalo songs solely to delight himself. But this time, when the buffalo came rolling down the hill it rolled right on top of Iktomi and trapped him facedown on the ground. Poor Iktomi lay half crushed and hardly able to breathe under the enormous weight of the large buffalo.

Surely I am going to die here! thought the frightened Iktomi. And he would have, but Iktomi has always been a lucky little man. This is really rather sad, for it has allowed him to continue in his foolish ways.

Again, luck was with Iktomi on this day. A pack of coyotes, curious to see what all the commotion was about—for a crashing buffalo makes a lot of noise—came to his rescue by eating the dead buffalo. Thus, Iktomi was set free.

The Spirits had punished Iktomi, but when he gained his freedom (thanks to the coyotes), he went triumphantly along his way. He was a bit sore and limping, to be sure, but that was a small price to pay for such power! Little did he know that the Spirits had taken the Buffalo Power from him.

A good way down the path, Iktomi came upon a small village. As he wandered around, the smell of buffalo stew coming from one of the tipis enticed him. Of course, Iktomi could not pass that by! So without so much as a greeting, he opened the tipi flap and entered. He could not see a thing, but he could hear someone stirring a pot. It was a very old grandmother, who was cooking up a wonderful stew for the hunters and their families, who would soon be home from a long (and hopefully good) hunt. For some reason known only to Iktomi and the darkness, he thought that the toothless grandmother was a beautiful young maiden, and his thoughts quickly turned from food to her. Lacking all propriety, Iktomi asked if he could kiss her!

Why not? thought the old woman. *It's been a long time since I've had a kiss.* So she said, "My young warrior, you may kiss me, for I am the loveliest women in our entire village."

Iktomi was so caught up in his own lust that he did not even recognize the voice of an old woman. He moved closer and embraced her, and she chuckled as he felt her deeply wrinkled skin and many warts. When he finally kissed the toothless old mouth, he thought that something must be dreadfully wrong.

"It is quite dark in here. Let me go outside and get some light," Iktomi said.

Outside the foolish one went, opening his buffalo-skin carrying bag and letting the sunshine illuminate the entire inside of the bag. The he quickly closed it, sure that he had trapped enough sunlight to see just who he was kissing inside of the tipi.

Inside the tipi he went, saying, "Now my beautiful maiden, it shall be as bright as day in here." He opened his bag full of sunlight, yet it remained as dark as it was before. Stymied, Iktomi left with disappointment written all over his face.

He had been walking for a long time since he left his village, and he was getting rather hungry. In fact, he realized that he was actually quite famished when he came across a pond full of ducks, who were leisurely swimming about and sunning themselves.

I am so hungry that I will just dive in and grab a few and eat them alive, Iktomi thought. But that was not Iktomi's way. He had to think of something clever, something that would net him a lot of ducks. Suddenly, an exquisite idea came to him. He rushed off into the woods to gather some grass that he rolled into a bundle with some leather he had. When the bundle was stuffed, he threw it over his shoulder and in a happy-go-lucky manner walked along the bank of the stream where the ducks could see him.

When the ducks saw Iktomi with such a large bundle over his shoulder, they became curious and called to him, "Brother, what do you have in such a large bundle?"

Iktomi pretended not to hear them. Instead, he slowly continued his walk by the bank but was sure not to leave the ducks' sight. Now, ducks are excitable and curious fellows, and they were oh-so-curious about the bundle. Soon they were quacking like mad, saying, "Please, brother, do not leave. Tell us what you have in such a large bundle."

As if he were really being inconvenienced, Iktomi stopped and said, "Ducks, I don't have time for you, so I suggest that you mind your own business. I must hurry to the next village."

Of course this just made the ducks all the more curious. "Why must you leave so quickly?" they asked.

"At the village there is going to be a feast and a great ceremony. I have been chosen above all others to be the singer for the dancing. The songs that I shall sing are all my own, and I carry them in this bundle," replied Iktomi. He gave his bundle a good thump, as if to say that inside lay his treasures. Then he turned to leave.

Naturally the ducks just got all the more excited and were quacking and quacking. "Please stay, just for a while! We all so want to dance and would love to hear your songs!" they cried.

Once again Iktomi pretended to be annoyed. "No, no. I must be moving on—enough of this," he said.

The ducks pleaded with Iktomi one more time, and he shrugged. "All right, all right. I'll sing just one song for you so that you may dance. I'll sing a very sacred ceremonial song, so you must listen carefully to my instructions and obey them all precisely. This very, very sacred song is called 'The Shut-Eye Song.' You are very lucky ducks, indeed, to hear it. I warn you, your eyes will turn to red coals if you open them and offend the spirits. So be sure to your keep eyes tightly shut until after the song is over," Iktomi explained.

The ducks were so happy to be able to dance to a new song that they cried out in unison, "Yes, yes, we understand! We shall follow any instructions you give us."

"All right, then. Shut your eyes tightly, and I shall begin," said Iktomi. He sang: "You must dance, you must dance/ With eyes tightly shut, you must dance!/ Yes, dance, dance with your eyes tightly shut/ If your eyes are open they shall become forever red/ So, dance, dance with your eyes tightly shut!"

The ducks did just as Iktomi had instructed them: They all danced around in a circle, carefully keeping time to the beat with their little eyes shut. And as they merrily danced, Iktomi began to knock them over the head, beginning with the fattest. So clever was Iktomi that his voice and his drum never missed a beat. However, there was one little duck who had not trusted Iktomi from the beginning, and he opened his eyes.

"Open your eyes!" he shouted. "Foolish ducks, Iktomi is trying to kill us all!"

Immediately all the ducks that Iktomi had not killed flew away, quacking for dear life.

Iktomi was quite satisfied, thinking, *Now that was a great plan—and quite successful, I might add! I have enough juicy ducks to last me for several days. Those ducks were so stupid!*

Since Iktomi had no reason to keep his "songs," he dumped them all and put the ducks in his leather bundle. Iktomi left the stream and looked for a pleasant place with shade to roast his ducks. He soon found a large tree that offered plenty of shade. Then he built a fire and let it burn down to the coals, put the ducks under the coals, and sat back, very self-satisfied as he contemplated the delicious meal that was soon to be ready. "Oh," he said, "those roasting ducks smell so wonderful that they are making me a bit sleepy, as if I had just eaten them all. I think I'll just take a little nap while they roast."

Iktomi tried to fall asleep, but for some reason he just couldn't seem to keep his eyes off the tasty ducks. Suddenly a strong wind started to blow, and it blew stronger and stronger until the trees were moving back and forth. A branch high up in the tree that he was camped under began to sway so that it started to rub another large branch from the tree next to Iktomi's. The noise was quite irksome, like two cats screeching at one another.

"Hey, brothers, stop that fussing!" Iktomi cried. "You are from the same family, so there is no need to quarrel." But the wind just blew harder and harder, making the screeching worse. The noise was annoying Iktomi more and more. So he climbed the tree in order to separate the branches when a large gust of wind came separating the branches quickly—and then they snapped back just as quickly, catching Iktomi's hand in between them.

As soon as this happened, the wind calmed down, leaving Iktomi stuck there in the tree . . . with the smell of roasting duck wafting up to torment his nostrils.

Since he was up so high, Iktomi could see for a great distance. He spied a coyote going this way and that, a sure sign that he was following the scent of something. He would trot along, his nose to the ground, then stop and sniff the air and move on. From his perch, Iktomi could tell that the coyote seemed a bit on the thin side and probably had not eaten for days.

The coyote did not seem to be able to fix upon any distinct scent, so he began to walk away from where Iktomi was caught high up in the tree. The foolish Iktomi, despite the coyote moving away from him, yelled out, "Coyote, don't you come over here! I am roasting plump, juicy ducks; and I have no intention of sharing them with anyone, much less a coyote."

The coyote looked around and saw Iktomi stuck up in the tree and said to himself, "So, my nose was right as usual—there *is* something mighty fine to eat over there."

Iktomi started yelling at the coyote, "Don't you dare come over here, the roasting ducks are mine! Go away this instant!"

The coyote, of course, did not listen. He could see that Iktomi was securely stuck between the branches, so he had quite a feast. He tore the ducks apart, savoring every juicy, warm morsel. Poor Iktomi could do nothing but drool and fume with anger.

The coyote was not a selfish fellow. Despite Iktomi's cursing him, the coyote said, "My brother, why don't you come down and enjoy this feast with me? There is plenty for the two of us. I would bring some duck to you, but you see, I have never learned to climb trees. So hurry on down before the ducks get cold. Come on, let's feast together!"

Iktomi could hardly bear to see his ducks being eaten. He was doubly upset because he had conceived of and carried out such a splendid plan to get them. As the coyote was getting his fill and feeling his tummy well satisfied, he thought, *I am about full, and the ducks do, in truth, belong to Iktomi. I think that I should leave him at least one or two—that seems only fair.* So he called up to Iktomi, "Brother, I am going to leave you a duck or two. Don't worry."

The coyote really did want to save some for Iktomi, but the ducks were so delicious that he just couldn't seem to make himself stop eating them. Finally, the coyote thought, *I'll just eat one more and leave the rest for poor Iktomi.*

The coyote began to uncover the coals so that he could find his one last duck, but there were none left. *Oh, goodness,* he thought, *I have eaten them all. How thoughtless of me! Well, Iktomi will probably understand; after all, he is a man of great character. He may not even be hungry at all after he finishes making peace between the two trees.*

It was such an enormous feast for the coyote that he decided he really needed a nap. He stretched himself out below the tree in which Iktomi was still caught on a soft mat of tufted grass and drifted into a most peaceful and satisfying nap. A few hours later, the coyote awoke refreshed and with his energy restored by the luscious duck meat. "Iktomi," he said, "I want to thank you for such a splendid feast. The next time that you have such a feast, please do not forget to invite your brother." With that, the coyote stretched and yawned and trotted away.

Not long after the satiated coyote left, a strong wind came up and blew the branches holding Iktomi apart. He pulled his bruised and throbbing hand out and scrambled down the tree. Iktomi was furious. He scattered the ashes and the coals, but there was not a duck to be found.

Iktomi set out to track down the coyote. One of the few things that Iktomi could do well and not botch was track. He carefully followed the coyote's footprints until he found him lying by a fire taking a nap, which, of course, coyotes love to do. As the coyote snored, Iktomi hid behind a large cottonwood tree making his plans. He thought, *Ha, ha, I have him now! I am going to kill and eat that devil. He will wish that he had never touched my ducks! Let's see . . . I will bash him in the head with my war club. No, that won't do. I like to eat brains the most, and I wouldn't want to ruin them for sure. Hmm . . . maybe I'll knock him as hard as I can in the ribs. That should do it! No, I love rib meat too much and I do not want to spoil them. So, how can I kill him and not hurt any of the meat I so enjoy? I know—I will find a large rock and tie it around his neck and throw him in the river! Ugh, no, that would ruin <u>all</u> the meat. And how would I ever get him back on land? Surely the river would carry him away. There has got to be a way. I know—I will pick him up and throw him in the fire and have a fine barbecue of coyote! Yes, that's what I'll do!*

The coyote had heard Iktomi coming. Probably everyone in the forest did, for he was cursing quite loudly as he followed the coyote's tracks. The coyote was not asleep at all—he was only pretending and had heard every word that

Iktomi had said. Iktomi quietly sneaked up on the coyote and grabbed him to throw him in the fire. But the coyote was no fool—he sprang out of Iktomi's grasp, ran to the river, and swam across to the far shore. When the coyote reached the top of the large hill across the river, he stopped to laugh at the foolish Iktomi—for when the coyote had jumped from his arms, Iktomi had fallen into the fire! The coyote watched as Iktomi brushed the ashes off and tried to soothe his fresh and smarting burns. Oh, was Iktomi angry now—and hungrier than ever. Once again he went on his pitiful way.

On and on Iktomi walked, cursing the coyote for feasting on his ducks and searching for something to eat. Eventually he came upon a patch of wild turnips and devoured them until he'd had his fill. *Not exactly duck,* he thought rather sadly, *but at least it's something.*

When the nourishing turnips renewed his strength, Iktomi continued on with still no destination in mind. Far down the forest path, he came upon a very large giant who was felling trees, but not in the way we would—he simply grabbed them tight and twisted, and up they came, roots and all. Or, if the tree was not too large, he would simply lay his mammoth hands upon it and push it over. Giants in those days were even stronger than they are now.

Iktomi walked over to where the giant was and asked, "Why are you uprooting all these trees? Can't you see that they are the very best in the forest? What could you possibly want with them?"

The giant replied to the impudent Iktomi, "Little fellow, these are all tall and straight trees, and they make wonderful arrows. That's why."

Of course Iktomi was always sure that he was smarter than anyone else, so he quite impolitely replied, "Come on! You are smarter than that, giant. The trees that you have knocked over are far too large for arrows."

Iktomi was sure that the giant must be a little off in the head and told him so. Well, despite their size and rough appearance, giants are rather sensitive creatures and have a strong distaste for humans meddling in their affairs. The giants of old had learned very early that if there was any creature of the forest that was stupid, it was those wasteful little two-leggeds who never seemed to be able to leave well enough alone. The giant was a bit annoyed with the unwanted company of Iktomi and told him so: "Listen, you impertinent little human, why don't you just continue on your journey. Can't you see that I am busy gathering up these fine arrow sticks?"

"They are not arrow sticks," countered Iktomi, "they are trees, you crazy giant!"

"Oh, please go away this instant. I have many more arrow sticks to gather before the sun sets," said the annoyed giant.

"Well," replied Iktomi, "if you really think that they are arrow sticks, then shoot one for me. In fact, shoot one *at* me!"

"Ugh! You are right next to me—you will have to move back a bit."

So Iktomi walked a good way from the giant into an open field. "No, no—that is still far too close," the giant snorted. Iktomi walked even farther away, at least 200 paces.

"Farther still," yelled the giant. "You might as well be sitting in my lap!" Iktomi walked even farther away, even though he must have been at least a mile from the giant by now and could hardly see him. Nevertheless, the giant could see Iktomi.

"All right, that's far enough," the giant's voice roared across the field. When Iktomi stopped, the giant picked up one of the trees and threw it at him, roots first. The tree did not move with the swiftness of a normal arrow, but as it moved through the air, it made an enormous thunderlike sound. Iktomi could see that the tree was coming straight for him, and he was gripped with fear. The almost deafening roar of the thunder only made his heart beat faster as he dodged this way and that, trying to get out of the path of the arrow-tree. It was of no use. No matter which way Iktomi ran, the tree followed him. It was as if the arrow-tree did not want to hit him too soon, but would rather torment him by following his every twisted turn. At last, Iktomi spied a rabbit hole and dove into it, but only his head would fit. There was poor Iktomi with his head stuck in the rabbit hole and his body flailing about outside of it. The arrow-tree crashed right into Iktomi's backside, separating his body from his head. His body flew through the air and landed far from his poor head, which was still stuck all by itself in the rabbit hole. Did the pitiful Iktomi ever cry out!

"Help me! Oh, help me please, I beg of you!" the distressed little man yelled.

The giant took his time walking over to where Iktomi's severed head was stuck. As the giant approached, Iktomi could hear his self-satisfied chuckling. "Well, well, what do we have here?" exclaimed the giant. "A talking head!"

"Giant, please have mercy on me! I beg of you to put my body and head back together again. I can't even walk home like this!" pleaded Iktomi.

Since giants do have tender hearts, the sight of this foolish man without a head touched his compassion.

"I am so sorry, little man. I did not mean to do this to you. Since you doubted my word, I had only hoped to show how a giant could shoot trees as if they were arrows. Let me go get my medicine bag and I will do my best to make you whole again," said the giant. In a short time, he returned with both his powerful medicine and Iktomi's body. He applied the sticky medicine to both Iktomi's neck and body, and soon they were joined as if they had never been separated.

"Well," said the giant, "that should do it! You're all one piece again. So, what do you think of my tree arrows now, little man?"

The ever-impudent Iktomi could only answer, "Someday, if you practice enough, you just might become an archer." And with that, Iktomi resumed his journey without so much as a thank you, but a very sore neck reminded him of his encounter with the giant and his arrow-trees for some time.

It had been a long and tiring day for Iktomi. His many misadventures had left him sore and exhausted. It was time for him to lie down and get some sleep. *Ugh,* he thought as he nestled in his buffalo robe, *there sure are a lot of foolish people on the Earth.* With that, he drifted into an uneasy sleep as scary dreams floated through his mind. At last the dreams awoke him. The moon was clear and bright that night, and at the end of his buffalo robe he could see the large hands of a ghost reaching for him.

"Get out of here!" screamed Iktomi. The large hands did not move from the end of the robe. Again, Iktomi screamed at the hands, "Go away! Don't make me have to get out of my cozy robe and send you away." The large hands did not move. Now Iktomi was getting distressed. How dare the ghost not even respond to him? "If you do not leave this very moment, I am going to get very angry," he said in the most threatening voice he could muster. The hands stayed where they were. "This is it! Either you leave right now or I am going to smash you with my war club! Don't think for a moment that I won't!" The large ghostly hands neither responded nor moved. That was enough. Iktomi grabbed his war club with its large, pointed stone, and with all the strength he had, smashed the hands.

"Ow, ow, ow!" cried Iktomi as he hopped about on one foot while massaging the toes of his other foot. You see, Iktomi had smashed his own foot. There was no ghost at all. But of course, the little Spider-Man could not be wrong, so he said, "Ugh, this is just not a good place to sleep!" and on he went.

And there you have a day in the life of Iktomi, a very, very foolish man indeed.

Chasing Deer: So, tell me, Grandson, what do think the story is about from the viewpoint of a Lakota? In many ways it seems obvious, but I think that for a non-Lakota, much of the story may not be so clear. However, with all our discussions over the past few days, I bet that you can see it as we would.

John: I'll give it a stab. To begin with, no Lakota man would ever approach a young woman as Iktomi did at the beginning of the story. Lakota women were very modest and were also expected to be treated with the greatest of respect as givers of life to the nation. No man would ever think of even laying his head upon his wife's lap in public. For a Lakota, Iktomi's behavior would be seen as outrageous, and the greatest scorn would have been heaped upon him.

Chasing Deer: Very good. Our women were seen as sacred beings requiring the utmost respect. Clearly you remember what happened to the lustful young hunter in the story of White Buffalo Calf Maiden. Go on, please. I am enjoying this!

John: I remember that the other morning we were discussing the contempt the Lakota warriors had for the soldiers of the United States because they took orders from another rather than make their own decisions. In Lakota culture, no one could make anyone do anything, much less demand it, not even a chief. Thus, if a warrior thought, for whatever reason, that he should not fight in a particular battle, that was his prerogative and it was respected. Each and every Lakota was morally autonomous. Again, Iktomi's demand that his head be cleared of lice by the young women would have brought him great contempt by others.

Chasing Deer: You have learned well, Grandson. A man who had his moral autonomy stripped from him by any so-called authority was no longer capable of acting as a man. There is only one authority: The Great Mysterious.

John: I take it that both his falling into the stream going after the berries and his attempt to capture the sunlight was just a way of pointing out that Iktomi was both a fool and not really a Lakota.

Chasing Deer: Why would these things point to him not being Lakota?

John: As you've pointed out to me, Grandfather, Lakota children were trained almost from birth to observe the natural world with great care. And as you also told me, becoming aware of all the senses was one of the things that a child was learning during her periods of sitting in silence. By the time a child was ten, she had an intimate knowledge of the natural world in which she lived.

Iktomi's next encounter with the deceased warrior shows egregious disrespect for the dead and, hence, the ancestors. The Lakota had enormous respect for the dead, as we saw in the Keeping of the Soul ceremony. They were quite conscious of the fact that they were only alive and had their religion and culture today because of the love of those who preceded them. On top of this, he lies to the dead warrior to hopefully ward off the ire he deserves.

Chasing Deer: You are truly beginning to understand us, *Mitakuye Oyasin*.

John: I see now why you called him sort of an antihero. Iktomi's behavior with the medicine man is full of unforgivable behavior. He lies to the medicine man and breaks his promise to him, he kills the buffalo to amuse himself, and he abuses a gift from the Spirits.

I know from our discussions that lying is just about the greatest "crime" that a Lakota could commit, and I feel sure that breaking a promise was right up there with it. The disregard for the lives of the buffalo is out of line, to say the least, with Lakota traditions and values. Furthermore, it flies in the face of "all my relations."

Chasing Deer: You are absolutely right about everything. In this story, Iktomi violates so many of the sacred values of the Lakota and shows himself to be totally self-centered, a trait despised by our People. Nothing is a "relation" to him; others are barely seen to exist for him other than as objects. As far as his total disregard for a gift from the Spirits, need anything be said?

John: Let me see . . . well, it seems to me that his behavior with the old grandmother is clear from what I have already said. He just does what he wants to without regard for anyone else.

I do not think that there is too much to say about the ducks and the coyote except that perhaps it is meaningful when the coyote says, "The next time that you have such a feast, please do not forget to invite your brother." It is the Lakota way to share, not to selfishly hoard as Iktomi was going to do. I am not sure that I understand the encounter with the giant except that Iktomi is very arrogant, another trait disliked by the Lakota. Of course, as usual he gets his "comeuppance," so to speak. Is there more, Grandfather?

Chasing Deer: Yes, there is, and it very important—but it would not be obvious to one raised outside of our culture, at least so it seems to me. If you think of the giant as a member of a different tribe or group, then what you see is the arrogant Iktomi making fun of something that he does not understand. We recognized that others had different ways and traditions, and we were taught to respect them. We knew that the Arapaho had their ways, the Hidatsa theirs, and so forth. We were who we were, and they were who they were, and that was fine. In fact, the first Making of Relatives Ceremony was between two tribes—the Arikara and the Lakota—not two people. This is why there were never any Indian religious wars as have occurred so frequently in your culture. Unlike Iktomi, the Lakota were taught to respect differences except when it came to moral right and wrong.

John: You're right. I would have never seen that in the story. It seems that almost everything Iktomi does boils down to disrespect. Would that be a fair statement?

Chasing Deer: Absolutely. If there is any word that typifies Indian culture it is *respect*. That is really all you need to know in almost all the Iktomi stories. You may note that Iktomi's parting words to the giant are quite disrespectful in spite of the giant having just saved his life. For a true Lakota, that act itself would have generated a lifelong gratitude toward the giant. All these things that we have talked about, the Lakota child knew by an early age. The stories just reinforced them in an amusing way.

Grandson, you have done very well in your comprehension of this story. I will give you an A.

John: Thank you, Grandfather.

Chasing Deer: But is something not amiss?

John: I don't know what you mean.

Chasing Deer: A Lakota parent or elder would never grade a child, for that sets up a comparison between him and others. This kind of competition was seen as unhealthy, since each child had his gifts to offer. Furthermore, the only, and I stress *only,* reward ever given a Lakota child was her or his sense of achievement. It is our strong belief that for a child to do anything for any kind of external reward was to chance the breeding of an unhealthy mind. So, Master John, I am taking my A back and throwing it in the fire where it belongs!

John: Oh no! I may not get into law school!

Chasing Deer: Think of it this way: I have done you a favor! Ready for another story? I promise that it will be a short one, and then I am taking these old bones to bed.

John: Sounds great!

CHAPTER FIVE

Iktomi
and the Hawk

Chasing Deer continued on with his stories of Iktomi, as John prepared to absorb another intriguing tale from his grandfather.

One fine day, Iktomi was taking a walk. He got a little tired, so he stopped and rested upon a log. Over him he saw a powerful hawk flying, doing loops, and just having a wonderful time.

That really looks like fun, Iktomi thought. So he called out, "Ho, brother hawk, why don't you come down here and give me a ride?"

The hawk was a friendly fellow, so he flew down and had Iktomi crawl upon his back. Up they went, higher and higher, and the views were magnificent. *This is really fun!* thought Iktomi, but before long he was bored. Poor little Spider-Man could never just enjoy something—his mind was always quickly dissatisfied, causing him to move on to something else.

Often he would break his boredom by playing a trick on someone. This time was no different, and soon he had thought of something to do. Every time another bird flew by, whether it was a mighty eagle or a little sparrow, Iktomi sent a gesture their way that indicated that the hawk was stupid and good-for-nothing. My, Iktomi was having fun!

What a fool everyone will think the hawk is, Iktomi thought. *This is great fun—the stupid hawk doesn't even know what I am doing!*

But the hawk was *not* stupid. He was watching the shadows upon the ground that he and Iktomi were casting as they glided about in the sky, so he had seen every indecent gesture that Iktomi had made. He thought, *I'll show that nasty little Spider-Man a thing or two for making a fool of me in front of my brothers.*

As soon as they flew over a forest, the hawk turned over and flew upside down—and off dropped Iktomi, who landed inside of a hollow, dead tree. And he could not seem to find his way out of the tree when it started to rain. The more it rained, the more the tree swelled. Soon it had soaked up so much water that Iktomi thought he would be crushed to death. He was so scared that he began to pray: "Oh, Great Spirit, You who made me so clever, why am I always getting myself into one jam after another? Every time I try to make a fool of someone, *I* am the one who gets fooled. I ask you, Great Spirit, to have pity on me. Please, *please* have mercy on me!"

For once the proud and haughty Iktomi humbled himself. He felt terrible about all that he had done during his life, and he felt like a very small person. In fact, he became so small that he was able to wiggle himself out of the tree. So, you can see what a little prayer and humility can do—even for a foolish person like Iktomi.

Chasing Deer: The meaning here should be easy for you to glean, I am sure.

John: Well, again it is about disrespect, which is only heightened here by the fact that the hawk was doing Iktomi a favor. Furthermore, it is very distasteful to a Lakota to do something behind another's back. It shows both disrespect and cowardliness, not to mention that it was in the worst of taste to ever make fun of another.

Chasing Deer: Yes! That answer deserves a feather, but now it is time for bed. I am sorry that you have to leave so soon, Grandson. I have truly enjoyed your company. Tomorrow night will be our last campfire together for a while.

John: I know, Grandfather. I'm eagerly looking forward to it!

CHAPTER SIX

Iktomi, Flint Boy, and the Grizzly Bear

The next night was as clear as any John had ever witnessed. After he and Chasing Deer had passed around the pipe, the young man again eagerly settled in to hear more fascinating stories from his grandfather's People.

Chasing Deer: Grandson, I have four more stories to tell you. I do not think that you will have any trouble at all getting their meanings. They all revolve around the Lakota values of tribal welfare: honesty, generosity, courage, individuality, humility, and, of course, respect.

John: I think that I've got a fair grasp of how to see the stories now within the context of your culture.

Chasing Deer: Good. Let us begin.

Iktomi was a very fortunate man to have a lifelong friend in Flint Boy. There were not many in the tribe who cared for Iktomi. Who would? After all, he was always up to trickery of some kind. Flint Boy was different—he was from the Inyan Wakan, the sacred stone nation that was Grandmother Earth's oldest and wisest creation. Aged stones learn compassion even for the foolish, and they are wise enough to know that to be compassionate is the only way to live in peace with oneself. Think about this: Have you ever seen a stone agitated or angry? Perhaps a young stone like Flint Boy could be pushed a little too far, but he would outgrow that in time. To put up with Iktomi, he was obviously growing into a mature stone quite successfully.

One fine spring day the two friends decided to take a trip to see some places that they had never seen before. As they journeyed along, they were both very excited about the new things that they might see and what adventures might come their way. All of a sudden, a giant grizzly bear appeared from behind a large oak tree. The friends knew that they were in trouble, for the bear looked quite menacing. The bear attacked, and Iktomi ran as fast as his legs could carry him to hide. Flint Boy, however, stood his ground. As the bear attacked him, Flint Boy dodged this way and that, taking every opportunity to stab the bear with his knife. At last the great grizzly fell dead before the unharmed Flint Boy.

It was only then that Iktomi came out of his hiding place. "What a display of courage and knifemanship! The tribe must know of this great thing that you have done," said the still badly shaken Iktomi.

"Think nothing of it, my friend," Flint Boy replied. "What is important is that neither of us were harmed. This is as large a grizzly bear as I have ever seen. Its coat will make a very cozy and warm blanket for my bed. Look at how enormous his claws are, Iktomi. They will become one fine bear-claw necklace, don't you think?"

"That is for sure," answered Iktomi. "I have never been so impressed as I was just now by your courage and skill. From this day forward, I will call you my little brother."

Now, any Lakota knows that a stone is not a little brother to anyone, especially not a human.

"No, Iktomi, you will not call me your little brother. I am so much older and I killed the bear. *You* are the little brother, and so shall I call you," said Flint Boy.

Iktomi would not accept this. How could he, Iktomi, be seen as less than anyone else? It was downright insulting. As they walked along, Iktomi continued to argue with Flint Boy as to who was the eldest brother. Even though Flint Boy's patience was wearing a little thin, he put up with Iktomi's complaining, knowing that it would eventually come to an end. When they finally arrived at a beautiful lake, Iktomi did indeed cease his whining.

"You are right, my friend, we have been so close for such a long time," Iktomi admitted. "It really doesn't matter to me what we call each other. So, I would like to call a truce."

"This is good," Flint Boy responded. "Let us vow to never quarrel again. It is very unpleasant to me and not something I am used to as I grow older."

"Friend, come on over here by the shore. I want to show you something," said Iktomi. "Come look at this enormous fish. It is the biggest one I have ever seen!"

Flint Boy, glad that Iktomi's focus had changed, walked over to the lakeshore to be with his friend. When he peered over the edge of the lake to see the fish, Iktomi stepped behind him—and with one gigantic shove, pushed Flint Boy into the lake. Of course, a stone cannot swim, so poor Flint Boy sank immediately to the bottom of the deep lake, never to reappear again. Even today, if you go to the lake you can see bubbles coming up from the very spot where Iktomi pushed Flint Boy in.

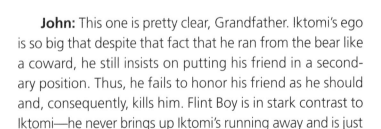

John: This one is pretty clear, Grandfather. Iktomi's ego is so big that despite that fact that he ran from the bear like a coward, he still insists on putting his friend in a secondary position. Thus, he fails to honor his friend as he should and, consequently, kills him. Flint Boy is in stark contrast to Iktomi—he never brings up Iktomi's running away and is just happy that both of them are safe; in return, Iktomi murders him. Yet the characteristics of Iktomi murder the tribe, so to speak.

Chasing Deer: That is exactly right. In every story that I have told so far, Iktomi's behavior is detrimental to the values that cement the society together, values that allow each member to selflessly contribute to the welfare of all. The beauty of the Lakota is that we were able to fuse the most extreme individuality with an overriding concern for the welfare of all.

John: That's surely something that Western civilization has never been able to do. We always see society and the individual in conflict. It's actually an amazing accomplishment when put against the best that we've ever been able to produce.

Chasing Deer: Quite right. Now are you ready for the Man-Eating Monster?

John: I'm all ears!

CHAPTER SEVEN

Iktomi and the Man-Eating Monster

Once again, Iktomi was out for walk. After all, you cannot find someone to trick or humiliate if you stay in your tipi all day, nor can you find any adventures that you can later brag about to the tribe. No, if you want to do these things, you need to get out into the world.

It was a fine spring day: The flowers were starting to bloom, and trees were growing their new leaves. As Iktomi walked along, he noticed an enormous rock that seemed almost as large as a small mountain. He thought, *That looks interesting. I think I will go have a look.*

As our trickster friend approached the rock, he saw a thick vine that went all the way from the top of the rock to the Earth below. Now, you can probably guess that Iktomi loved to climb vines. In fact, he could resist them no more than he could resist buffalo stew. So, Iktomi grabbed hold of the vine, changed himself into a spider, and scampered up the vine with all eight of his legs.

What Iktomi did not know was that at the top of the rock lived the fearsome Man-Eating Monster. So, when Iktomi reached the top, he quickly realized that this was one vine he wished that he had never climbed. "Oh, why did I turn myself back into a man at the top of the vine? If I were still a spider, that monster would probably not even notice me. Well, it is too late now," Iktomi said to himself.

But Iktomi never lost his wits easily, so he greeted the frightful-looking beast like this: "*Hau,* little brother. I have been looking for you all day."

The monster did not care for this intrusion, but his mouth *was* beginning to water, so he replied, "I have not had much to eat for the past few days."

"That is awful, little brother," said Iktomi. "But do not worry—in a few hours it will be time for dinner."

"Dinner! I have not even had breakfast! I am hungry right now, and I bet you would be quite tasty roasted with a few onions," growled the monster.

"You do not want to eat me, little brother. You see how puny and hairy I am—why, I would not even be a mouthful for you," Iktomi quickly replied.

"Who are you, anyway?" the angered Man-Eating Monster asked. "And do not insult me by calling me little brother. I am no little brother of yours, you ugly two-legged!"

"Oh, really? Tell me, when did you come to the Earth?" responded Iktomi.

"What, you fresh little man? I was born *with* the Earth," the monster said. "Are you stupid? All monsters were born when the Earth was made, don't you know that?"

"Well, I am sorry, monster, but it was I, Iktomi, who made the Earth," Iktomi replied. "I also made the moon, the sun, and all the heavens. And, as I remember, I made you, too. In fact, when I made you I was very disappointed because you were so small and ugly that I just discarded you then and there."

Now, if you are a two-legged, one good thing to know about monsters is that they are not very smart and are quite gullible. Having made them, Iktomi knew this.

Man-Eating Monster said, "It seems that you are right— you *are* older. I should call you my older brother, so I will. *Hau,* big brother, although you are pretty puny and I am still going to eat you. Even a little mouthful is better than nothing when you are as hungry as I am."

"Not so fast! As you said, I am not even worth the time to chew," the quick-witted Iktomi shot back. "I know where there is a whole village of very fat people who would be mighty delicious and filling! How about I show you where the village is, and then you can eat half of them while I eat the other half? We can be there in a few minutes. Doesn't that sound much better, little brother?"

Man-Eating Monster said, "That *does* sound much better, older brother. Let us go!" And with that, he ran down the mammoth rock so fast that when he got to the bottom he had to take a deep breath. It was so strong and deep that little Iktomi was nearly sucked into the monster's lungs.

"Whew! Please breathe the other way," said Iktomi.

"I am so hungry!" Man-Eating Monster explained. "I want to get to the camp! Come on, older brother—show the way."

"I'm starving, too, younger brother, so we should hurry along. But before we do, I need to know what you are scared of," said Iktomi.

"That is none of your business," said the monster with a twinge of anger. "Why do you want to know *that?*"

"I am just trying to look out for you, younger brother. I need to be sure that there is nothing at the village that would keep you from what is going to prove to be a most tasty meal," said Iktomi.

"Oh, well, that is a different matter. I thank you for look-ing after me—you truly are an older brother. I have never told anyone this before, but there are three things that scare me to death: a woman on her moon [a menstruating woman], a rattle, and a whistle. I do not know why, but they frighten the daylights out of me," admitted Man-Eating Monster.

As they hurriedly went on, their mouths began to water. (Well, at least the monster's was.) When they got close to the village, Iktomi stopped and told Man-Eating Monster, "You wait here. I will check out the village to be sure that there is nothing about to scare you. I do not want you to miss this feast!"

"Fine," said Man-Eating Monster. "Just make it snappy—I am famished!"

Iktomi hurried off to the village, glad to be away from such a ferocious beast. When he arrived, he had the chief call

all the people together. Iktomi told them, "I have terrible news. That insatiable Man-Eating Monster is headed this way right now. In fact, he is right outside the village, and I can tell that he is ravenously hungry. I am sure that he intends to eat each and every one of you. You know how voracious he is. But, do not worry—I, Iktomi, know how to scare the beast so that he will not dare set foot in the village. Is there a woman here on her moon?"

A young lady raised her hand, and Iktomi told her, "I want you to get a rattle and a whistle. When Man-Eating Monster appears, step out in front of him, blow your whistle, and shake your rattle. That will scare him so badly that he will turn around faster than you have ever seen a monster run in your life. And I can promise you that he will never return to this village. Now get ready, for he will be here soon."

Iktomi left and hurried back to where Man-Eating Monster was waiting in the woods just outside the village. Iktomi told him, "It is okay, little brother. There are no whistles, no rattles, and, to be sure, no menstruating women around for miles and miles."

"Thanks, older brother. That was most thoughtful of you," replied Man-Eating Monster. "I can tell that you are a fair two-legged, but there is something that I must tell you. You are so puny that there is no way you can eat half the people in the village. I am only going to let you have one or two of them. It is not nice to be greedy, you know."

"You are right," Iktomi agreed. "How about if I just have one?"

"You are not only fair but sensible as well, big brother," said Man-Eating Monster.

So Iktomi and the monster proceeded to the village. The monster could not wait, so he charged out in front of Iktomi. Yet just as he entered the village, the woman jumped in front of him, shaking her rattle and blowing her whistle as if she were mad. Man-Eating Monster was so startled that he literally died of fright right then and there.

So that is how Iktomi killed Man-Eating Monster, which he himself had made . . . if you can believe that!

Chasing Deer: I like that story. It is nice to see Iktomi use his wits for a good purpose for a change.

John: Yes, the little braggart is quite clever when his back is up against the wall, isn't he?

Chasing Deer: Old Iktomi is never lacking in brains, just values. The next story I will tell is one in which Iktomi ends up doing a good deed through his cleverness. He starts out being his normal old self, but in the end he gains redemption.

John: This should be interesting: a redeemed Iktomi.

CHAPTER EIGHT

Iktomi Becomes a War Hero

Iktomi was not a warrior; in fact, battles scared him to death. Besides being dangerous, fighting was wearisome due to little sleep, there was often not enough to eat, and it was physically and emotionally exhausting. But there was one appeal: When a warrior came back from a battle, he was expected to tell the gathered tribe of his exploits, which was a sure path to honor and respect.

As everyone knows, Iktomi was an habitual braggart. Whether there was any truth to his tales or not mattered little to him as long as he got what he wanted. So, despite his cowardice, when Iktomi turned of age he sought to go on a war party. He was sure that the honor and respect he might garner was worth the fear he might feel.

A group of rambunctious young warriors wanting to prove their mettle decided to form a raiding party to attack the Crow for some horses and whatever other valuable articles they might find. It was a sort of late adolescent initiation—the intent was not to kill anyone, but rather to display one's stealth and cunning and return unharmed. As the young men were preparing to go, one of them in jest asked Iktomi to go with them. To the group's surprise, Iktomi accepted the offer with his usual display of false bravado.

"What have we done?" one of the young warriors said. "That oaf Iktomi is afraid of a puppy dog. Can you imagine him face-to-face with an angry Crow? Look, Dancing Bear, you asked him, so you need to go and talk him out of going. He will be a real burden and danger to us all—we simply cannot have that whimpering coward along with us."

Dancing Bear went to talk to Iktomi. He was sure that if he made the raid sound dangerous enough Iktomi would change his mind. He was wrong. The more dangerous Dancing Bear portrayed the raid, the more Iktomi boasted of the manly feats that he was going to perform. It was useless—Iktomi was going to go, no matter what Dancing Bear or anyone else said.

The Lakota warriors' journey to the Crow village took many days. After about a week of clandestine marching, the scout came back and told the group that the village they sought was just over the next hill. The young warriors found a dense thicket of brush and trees to hide in while they finalized their raiding plans from the information that the scout had brought back.

The plan was simple: That night, under the cover of darkness, the warriors would find a place to hide just outside of the village. At sun's first light, while the village was still fast asleep, they would charge in with bloodcurdling war cries, throwing the people there into panic and confusion. The young men would be able to grab the best ponies and make their getaway before the Crow gathered their sleepy wits.

The next morning, Iktomi and his compatriots left their hideout and crept quietly toward the village. What they did not know was that a Crow scout had spotted them earlier, so the village was waiting for them to arrive. When the warriors entered the village with their cries, they were greeted by a large force of Crow warriors readied for battle. The Lakota war party had no choice but to retreat as quickly as possible. As fast as they galloped away, the Crow gained ground with their fresh and rested ponies. It did not take long before there were Crow arrows flying all around them. However, the brave Lakota warriors on the faster of the ponies counterattacked one at a time. They were eager for honor and wanted their slower brothers to be able to gain ground on the ever-advancing Crow warriors.

It took about three days for the young Lakota war party to finally lose the Crow. But there *were* losses: Some lay dead upon the moving battlefield and others had been captured. So, hungry and exhausted, they finally arrived at their village. Although some could see the excursion as a failure, the warriors were greeted by whoops of approval when they entered the center of the village. They were given a full heroes' welcome with dancing and feasting on buffalo.

When all had had their fill, the young warriors were taken to the large reception lodge, where seats of honor awaited them. Each warrior told his story amid the cheers and approval of the tribe, for their heroic actions had been admirable amid a most difficult situation. It was only natural (and expected, I might add) that there would be some exaggeration in some of the stories. At the height of the story, or when a particularly brave act was related, you could hear the women holler, the men shout their war cries, and the thunder of the drums. A group of warriors back from a raid was a time of excitement.

Soon it was Iktomi's turn to tell of his brave deeds and self-sacrifice in what was becoming a battle to be remembered. Iktomi was never at a loss for words—he could weave a story out of whole cloth in an instant. The crowd quickly became engrossed in his remarkable story and the shouts and drums were even louder than ever.

Iktomi described in the most vivid language how when the Crow had caught up with their war party and an ignominious defeat was at hand, he alone had held them off so that his brothers could escape and reassemble for the next phase of the battle. It was more than clear that had Iktomi not singlehandedly held off the enemy, it was unlikely that any of them would have returned home. It was obvious to all gathered that Iktomi's bravery and fortitude were legendary. Some, however, knew better. There was an occasional cry of "You cowardly mouse!" but the cheering crowd drowned these voices out. Oh, it was a glorious tale!

The moment Iktomi ended his story of courage, the other young braves stepped in and immediately revealed the truth of Iktomi's role in the attempted raid and retreat. While it was true that some braves had held off the Crow singlehandedly with great courage, Iktomi was not one of them. No, the truth was that Iktomi was so frightened that he froze. In order to save him from either death or capture, two other braves had had to pick Iktomi up and carry him to safety away from the battle.

Iktomi became the reddest Indian that you have ever seen. He ran from the assembly lodge after he had been tattooed with swinging breechclouts [loincloths], the sign of dishonor and contempt. His attempt to portray himself as the bravest of warriors was an utter failure, so Iktomi ran to the woods to suffer his humiliation in private. He was shattered. He was no warrior; in fact, he did not even deserve the name of Lakota.

How am I ever going to regain my status in the tribe? Iktomi wondered. *When they find me, I will probably be banned. Oh, what have I gotten myself into this time! And what can I possibly do now?*

Iktomi left the tribe and wandered about for months. As he journeyed, his mind was obsessed with one question: What could he do to show that he was a warrior? A man without a tribe is a miserable creature, and Iktomi was indeed extremely lonely.

While sitting under a large cottonwood tree going over his situation again and again, an answer came to him: All by himself he would gather warriors and create his own war party. Then he would find the Crow and avenge the retreat and his own humiliation. This would not be an easy task to be sure, but Iktomi was determined to erase the dishonor from his name. For days he thought about how to accomplish his plan. He thought about the weapons his war party would need, he thought about strategy, and he thought about what makes a good war chief.

Iktomi set out to recruit his war party. Yet, even though he was very determined, he had no luck at all. For months he searched for recruits and could not find even one. It took a long time for him to become discouraged, but finally, with head bowed, he headed for his home village.

As he trudged home in quiet despair, he happened upon a mud turtle. He convinced the creature to take a rest and talk to him. After the turtle was comfortable in his presence, Iktomi presented him with his plans for a raid of a scale never seen before. To his surprise, the mud turtle seemed interested and even started to augment his plans. The creature was all for the idea. After all, war and fame go together, so it was a good bargain for a lowly turtle.

The mud turtle and Iktomi agreed to an alliance. Then they sat down to eat and promised full allegiance to each other. This was followed by speeches of bravado and invincibility. Then the new friends danced around the campfire shouting war cries, as their excitement about the adventure grew.

After a hearty breakfast the next morning, the war chief and his lone warrior set out to find more soldiers for this most noble cause. Down the trail a bit they came upon a turkey, and Iktomi said, "Brother, come and council with us."

They did not have to council for long, for the turkey thought that Iktomi's plan was a splendid one. "Count me in," he said. "My life has become rather ordinary and wearisome. What I need is some excitement, an adventure."

The next to join the growing war party was a butterfly. He was a little wary of going to war against such a mighty enemy, but, as you know, Iktomi had a way with words— so before long, the timid butterfly was the fourth member of the group.

Iktomi's war party was an unusual assortment, to say the least. He would have liked some snakes, bees, black widows, scorpions, or mosquitoes because they all carried their own weaponry. The truth is, he was not sure about his motley crew. After all, how was he going to supply them with weapons?

As the group marched along toward where Iktomi thought the Crow must be, they met a skunk. Skunks are such timid fellows that the glib Iktomi had no trouble convincing him to join the others. They were now an awfully strange-looking war party!

Iktomi was learning how to be a war chief. He realized that the troops were getting restless, so he led them onward at a faster clip in order to raise their anticipation and have them keep their focus. He did not want any discord among such an odd collection of warriors. At night around the campfire, he fueled their imaginations with heroic exploits to be done and images of the Crow running for their lives with their tails between their legs.

Nevertheless, the long march was getting to the warriors, and bickering did break out. We all know what belligerent characters turkeys can be. Well, before long, he was aiming his sharp tongue at the turtle: "You are so slow, turtle," he harangued, "that you are holding us up from deeds of valor. Not only that, but you smell, too!"

"Well, Mr. Scabby Head, your neck is so scrawny that I do not know how you keep your pinhead from falling off," retorted the turtle.

It was not much better with the others and, of course, no one wanted to get near the skunk. They even made the poor fellow sleep away from the main encampment at night.

All of this was wearing Iktomi down. *How can I fight a battle without unity and harmony among my warriors?* he thought. In fact, he was about to give up on the entire plan altogether when he was sure that they had entered enemy territory. This news picked up everyone's spirits and changed their focus from each other to the battle at hand.

I said Iktomi was learning how to be a war chief. Well, there was progress, but he still had a lot to learn for sure. For example, the first night that they camped in enemy territory, he forgot to appoint a lookout. So, the next morning at sunrise, the crew found themselves surrounded by a group of fearsome Crow, who were not happy with this incursion into their homelands. The entire war party was captured without a single arrow flying. The Crow marched Iktomi and his crew back to the village, where they held a council to decide the fate of the captives.

"That's the strangest-looking war party I have ever seen," said the war chief. "There is no sense in adopting them into the tribe, as I do not know of what possible service they could be. Let us have some fun with them. After all, they came with the intention of doing us great harm."

A warrior was sent to get Iktomi. He roughly pulled the Spider-Man to his feet and dragged him to the war chief's tipi. However, the war chief was even rougher with Iktomi. He grabbed Iktomi by the scruff of the neck and shook the living daylights out of him.

"All right, you puny little mouse, you had better tell me what scares each of your men," the intimidating fellow demanded. "I have been a war chief long enough to know that even the most courageous of warriors have their fears. If you tell me, perhaps I will spare your life . . . or perhaps I won't. If you do not tell me, I will throw you over that cliff right now. Speak, you quivering little rodent!"

Iktomi was so scared that he could hardly open his mouth. His knees were shaking and his heart was pounding, but he gathered his wits as best he could. He actually gathered them rather well, for Iktomi was at his best when he had to use his craftiness to get out of a jam. "Chief, you know I cannot do that," Iktomi replied. "I am also a war chief, and it would be the greatest of betrayals to tell such things to an enemy. My conscience and my sense of honor would never allow me to do such a traitorous thing. But, on the other hand, if you will spare my life, I will tell you what you want to know.

"You are right, chief. Each of my men has one great fear and one great fear alone. I could tell you how to turn their legs to warm butter and have them wet their pants. How would that be, my chief?"

"That's what I want to know, mousy. Now out with it," implored the war chief.

"All right, I will tell you all. Believe me, my turkey is about as fearless as any warrior I have ever seen, but there is one thing that scares him badly. He cannot stand heights. If you want to turn him into a sniveling coward, just take him to a high cliff and push him off.

"My turtle warrior is so afraid of water that he never even washes. Just look at how muddy he is. The very thought of water starts him shaking from head to foot. If you want to see him whimper like a puppy, take him to a deep pond and throw him in.

"My butterfly warrior may look fragile to you, but believe me, he is very tenacious and as fast as a wild horse. There is, however, one thing that makes him shutter and freeze with fight, and that is the sound of arrows whizzing by him.

"My skunk warrior is really not much of a warrior at all, I am sorry to say. Skunks are about as timid and shy as can be. In fact, did you know that they are so shy that they only come out at night? And their shyness is nothing compared to their modesty! I will tell you the truth, my war chief: If you lifted up the tail of that skunk and put your head under it, why, he would die of shame that instant! I am not joking, just give it a try. I would save him for last, if I were you, because you will laugh all night long!"

Iktomi had done it. He had broken the code of honor of every war chief by revealing the weakness of his men.

The Crow grouped again for a conference. Then they broke up and with hair-raising screams ran over and grabbed the poor turtle, pulling him by his stubby tail toward a nearby pond. The turtle resisted with all his might, digging his claws deep into the ground. But it was no use, for the warriors were too strong and too driven. The turtle screamed, pleading for his life. Yet the more he yelled, the more determined the warriors became until at last they had him by the edge of the deep pond. They hoisted him up and tossed him far out into the pond. It was sad to watch. For a while the turtle managed to keep his head above water, but soon he lost the struggle and sank like a stone. The warriors let out cries of delight.

Iktomi's warriors huddled together, horrified at the undignified manner in which the Crow had dispatched their comrade. They knew that they would all meet a similar fate, yet the terror on their faces only served to energize the crazed Crow. Next, they grabbed the turkey and pulled him by the neck toward the nearby cliff. The more the turkey fought, the angrier the warriors got.

"Please let me go! If you do, I promise to tell you how to give Iktomi the most undignified death of all," the turkey begged.

But it was all to no avail. The warriors just laughed at him and continued to drag him closer to the cliff's uppermost ledge. There they gave him a mighty push. The turkey plummeted over the edge, and the warriors danced with glee. About halfway down, the turkey opened his wings and flew away. The warriors were too busy dancing and whooping to even notice the turkey's escape.

The Crow went back to the two remaining warriors. This time they decided to have their way with the butterfly, who pleaded for some mercy. "Warriors, I can do no harm," he said. "Why do people always have to fight with each other? We of the butterfly nation spend our time spreading beauty and happiness wherever we go."

The warriors could not have cared less. They were in no mood to hear about beauty and happiness. "What will be beautiful and bring us great happiness is to see our enemy ignominiously dispatched!" they said.

With their position clear, the warriors began to fire their arrows at the little butterfly. But they could not even come close to bringing a shot home. The agile little soldier would quickly zoom out of harm's way—he went up in the air, down to the ground, flying left, and diving right. You simply could never tell where he would be from one instant to the next. It was a useless task for the warriors, and soon they were out of arrows. More astonished than angry, they watched as the butterfly flew high in the air and soon became a speck far in the distance before disappearing.

The Crow knew that something was wrong. The butterfly had dodged the arrows of even their best marksmen as if they had never shot a bow before, and then he got cleanly away. They were cursing and hopping mad when they went to get Iktomi.

"You lying little mouse! If there is anything else that is amiss, you will suffer! You will be scalped alive and burned at the stake! Do you hear me, you little liar?" shouted the war chief in Iktomi's face.

Next they began to kick the skunk and abuse him in every way imaginable. Then the warrior chief remembered what Iktomi had told them about the skunk's one great fear and his curiosity was aroused.

"Stop! Let us surround him and really humiliate him," the chief ordered.

The warriors made a circle around the poor skunk and began to throw one insult after another at him.

"You loathsome, ugly coward! You are nothing more than a four-legged child, so modest that you wear your dress down to your ankles," the warriors taunted him. (I will spare you the worst of what they had to say.)

"Eagle Wing," the war chief said, "go and lift the little varmint's tail up."

The warriors knelt closely around the skunk while Eagle Wing pulled his tail up as hard as he could . . . and he was the first to be hit with the skunk's eye-burning spray. Eagle Wing let go of the tail immediately, as the skunk whirled on his front paws and targeted each warrior with remarkable accuracy. The warriors, blinded, were all rolling on the ground in horrific pain amid a stomach-wrenching odor.

Iktomi and the skunk made their getaway, but not before they had gathered up all the Crow's horses and galloped away from their victory.

When Iktomi and the skunk arrived home followed by several hundred Crow horses, the village cheered. This time, Iktomi was given a hero's welcome. The festivities lasted far into the night, and no matter how many times Iktomi and the skunk told their heroic tale, someone had to hear it again. At about sunrise, Iktomi and the skunk finally got to bed too tired to even take from their hair the coveted eagle feathers they had been adorned with.

So you see, cleverness can be used to good purpose.

Chasing Deer: There you go—a redeemed Iktomi!

John: I really liked that story, Grandfather. It was quite clever.

Chasing Deer: It also has a lesson in it for us.

John: I think you're talking about more than just Iktomi's perseverance and will, right?

Chasing Deer: Yes. What the Lakota would see in the odd assortment of characters that make up Iktomi's army and their subsequent means of escape was this: Each and every individual has his or her unique talents and abilities to bring to the overall well-being of the tribe. No tribal member was thought of as useless.

Now, Grandson, I am going to tell you two more stories and then you had better get to bed, for it is a long journey out of here. I think that you have learned enough about Iktomi and his wily ways that we need not discuss these stories. Rather, I am going to let you ponder them as you travel home. So, without further ado, let us get to the next story.

CHAPTER NINE

Iktomi's Marriage and Love Life

When Iktomi was barely into his physical manhood, he decided that he wanted to marry. This was unheard of, for he had not proven himself as a warrior, a provider, or a man. More important, even though he was intellectually precocious, Iktomi had yet to display the moral qualities that the other young men of his age had acquired. You see, long before puberty, a Lakota boy-child has the first lessons of childhood firmly embedded in his soul. These first lessons were silence, which we considered the cornerstone of all virtue; reverence; love; and self-restraint. By puberty, the qualities of generosity, courage, fortitude, and chastity were an essential part of a Lakota boy's character. There were other virtues, of course, such as humility, respect for elders, and a deep soulful recognition of the interrelatedness of all life.

Iktomi had developed none of these noble traits—instead, he was arrogant, insipid, and quite full of himself. Worse still, he lacked all ambition to become a man as defined by the Lakota virtues. He even held in disdain those boys his age that worked so hard at attaining manhood. Yet he wanted to marry!

Iktomi's father talked to him about his folly, pointing out his immaturity and the fact that he had accomplished none of the things required for Lakota manhood. Iktomi's ears remained closed, as they always did when it came to something he either did not want to hear or that went against his desires or plans. Instead, the ever-clever and glib Iktomi subtly switched tactics with his father, telling him a teaching story that he hoped would make it hard for his father to deny the rightness of his desire to marry.

Without giving his father's admonishments a moment's thought, Iktomi replied, "Father, you surely remember the story of the young warrior spirit who still sings a love song, don't you? An unfulfilled love song it is, for he died in battle at a young age. By seeking glory and recognition in a war that he did not have to fight in, he lost his life. He never got to experience the full joy and pleasure of being a young man. So, in his vainglory, he sought the ephemeral values of tribal adulation and honor—ephemeral because they were sought for and not gained from proper motivation. He now spends eternity bemoaning the loss of the fullness of his youth.

"Father, the elders have always said that one must take full advantage of one's youth, for that is the best of life's stages. One must devour every moment of it and live as fully as possible."

Iktomi cleverly paused, in the hopes that the wisdom of his story would become clear to his father. He then added, "It is only reasonable that I should have my enjoyments and delights at this time in life. When I am older, I will seek out brave deeds to perform, along with those other things that bring one standing and respect in the tribe."

Iktomi's father found this line of reasoning to be quite mature and sensible, so he was silent and said no more.

The little Spider-Man was only 14 and was undergoing those changes that puberty brings, including a voice that would range from high to low. And he was also experiencing new and unusual feelings, which, while certainly pleasant, filled him with some apprehension as well. For instance, he could not take his thoughts away from a bashful and beautiful maiden in the village whom he thought about day and night.

Although Iktomi was certainly not a warrior—nor had he even learned to hunt as the other boys his age had—that did not bother him in the least. He knew what he wanted, and he was going to get it. Convention and propriety were for others, not him. Everyone in the village knew that he had no more business seeking a wife than a child did. And since it was always the woman's choice as to who would be her husband, the People were sure that Iktomi's advances would be strongly rejected. This, they hoped, would bring the boy to his senses and set him on a course of learning the skills of manhood so that *one day* he would be able to have a wife. But they underestimated the clever Iktomi!

When our young friend was with the object of his desire, his words were smooth and romantic. He knew just the right things to say to make her feel faint and to make her heart flutter. It was not long before Iktomi's sweet talk and presumed profundity won the beautiful maiden's heart. When the marriage festivities were over, Iktomi and his bride went off into seclusion as newlyweds still do. And then they moved in with her mother.

Iktomi's mother-in-law was quite beautiful. She had been widowed as a young woman when her husband, a very brave warrior, did not return from a battle; and she had chosen to remain unmarried, despite the courtship of many fine Lakota men. Now she, her daughter, and Iktomi began their life together in this woman's tipi—which was not easy for Iktomi, thanks to his disdain for social traditions and Lakota propriety. You see, the manner in which one related to one's mother-in-law was quite formal and very strict. There was to be no outward familiarity between them; indeed, a son-in-law was not even to face his mother-in-law, much less talk to her. The only exception was if an emergency should occur.

Yet, from the time he first laid eyes on her, Iktomi felt the strongest of physical attractions to his mother-in-law. She was, after all, a most beautiful and elegant woman. As would have been customary, the newlyweds should have moved into their own tipi as soon as they could make one. And to be fair to poor Iktomi, he did try at first to abide by social custom.

But as his infatuation and desire for his mother-in-law grew, he soon had no intention of allowing custom and tradition to get in his way. He was quite happy with his living arrangements, as he was able to spend so much time in the presence of his mother-in law. As usual, Iktomi could not control his desires. After all, he was Iktomi! He defied all social customs, put his needs and wants above all else, and saw himself as above and better than others. In short, he was the very personification of what it was like *not* to be a Lakota.

Soon Iktomi's desire for his mother-in-law became an obsession. His lovemaking with his new bride became intense and passionate, but not because of his love for her—instead, Iktomi was trying to bury his uncontrolled passion for her mother! To his credit, he did hope that in time a closer relationship with his bride would diminish his lust for his mother-in-law, but it was not to be. Things got worse, and soon Iktomi was imagining himself being with his mother-in-law rather than his wife. His lovemaking had become dishonest, while his longing grew more intense.

The foolish boy's sexual obsession with his mother-in-law grew ever worse. He hated being away from her; in fact, Iktomi planned his days so that he would be home as much as possible without arousing too much suspicion or disdain for shirking his manly responsibilities. He even went so far as to often pretend to be ill, just so he could stay in the tipi with the object of his desire—and then he would lie in his bed imagining how wonderful it would be to touch her (or more).

As Iktomi watched his mother-in-law go through her daily chores, he was always hoping to catch a glimpse of her thigh should she stoop down for something. It took all of his willpower and resolve to control himself, and before long this game had taken its toll—Iktomi was becoming exhausted. He knew that he had to devise a plan.

Iktomi was smart enough to know that he was on dangerous ground, for if something happened between him and his mother-law-law, he would be in great trouble with the tribe. In fact, he was risking being banned from the village altogether. Nevertheless, after weeks of pondering his situation, Iktomi came up with a rather elaborate and ingenious plan. In order for it to work, he would have to carry out a series of well-orchestrated deceits. This, of course, was no problem for Iktomi . . . it was what he did best!

The impetuous Iktomi always had the greatest self-control and will when it came to carrying out a course of action that would get him what he wanted; thus, he began his plan. Soon the antisocial Iktomi began to take part in tribal affairs, claiming a newfound interest and dedication. *At last,* the People thought, *Iktomi is becoming a man.* Everyone was pleased with his new sense of tribal responsibility and involvement, and his mother-in-law was particularly happy that he was not constantly in the way in the tipi.

Iktomi's bride was taking pride in her husband's growing maturity (despite having no interest in tribal civic matters herself), but before long, Iktomi was hardly home at all. Every day he would give his wife some excuse for his being gone. Always, to be sure, it was an excuse that would hopefully convince her of his importance in tribal affairs and of his dedication to the welfare of the tribe. Yet he was not just gone much of the day—he would often be gone late into the night as well. Naturally his new bride was not happy with his constant absence, and like any Lakota woman would, she expressed her feelings about his overwhelming zeal.

To soothe his wife's growing discomfort with his daily absences, Iktomi told her that he had become involved with the Fox Society and was attending all their meetings. How he ever got the poor woman to believe this is a mystery! The Fox Society was made up of young warriors who had proven their courage and strength in battle, which Iktomi had surely not done. The clever one, of course, always had an answer—saying that he was a much sought-after guest due to his involvement in tribal matters. He also told his wife that if he were chosen to be a member, it would give her and the family quite a bit of prestige. After all, many chiefs came from the Fox Society, and who knows what honors might come to him from being a member of such a revered group? Feeling that he had more than satisfactorily answered his wife and that she would surely see the wisdom his of reasoning, Iktomi continued on his course.

Iktomi's wife, however, began to suspect that he was seeing another maiden. When he came home at night, she thought that he carried an unfamiliar scent, and she was certain that he was spending his nights with someone else. She was so sure, in fact, that she ceased any physical relationship with Iktomi. Lakota women will not put up with unfaithfulness, which, fortunately, was a rare event.

When they were courting, Iktomi's wife found his blundering, childish ways to be somewhat endearing. They were no longer that way to her. She was seeing him as he really was: a lying, conniving, cheeky braggart. She began to tell him exactly what she thought of him, going so far as to refer to him by names that were quite disrespectful. It actually brought her great satisfaction to see the little snake in the grass grovel and wince. The names she called him were certainly appropriate—had she known just how appropriate, she would have put his belongings outside the tipi [a simple act that denoted divorce for a Lakota woman].

Of course, Iktomi reacted to his wife's behavior quite strongly, child that he was. He would take his blanket and go to the top of hill and sit there for a good part of the day licking his smarting wounds. But to say that he was remorseful would be giving Iktomi far too much credit—no, he just did not like his plans being interfered with. Even so, his young and naive wife began to feel sorry for her husband, wondering if perhaps she had been too hard on him. Iktomi knew that she would do this, so he waited. Sure enough, she allowed her tender, womanly emotions to turn to guilt. To assuage these feelings, she would greet Iktomi when he came home in her finest clothing, with her hair braided and the subtle scent of fine oils upon her face. Then she would cook him a most delicious meal and want to know all about the Fox Society and the intricacies of tribal affairs and civic matters. Of course, she was only setting the stage for Iktomi to be able to continue with his mischievous plan.

Iktomi was wise enough, if one wants to call his scheming wisdom, to let things rest in peace for the time being
while he allowed his wife's confidence in him to restore itself.
He was sure that between her guilt and the kindly emotions
and behavior it generated toward him, he would soon be
able to resume his crafty and loathsome plan. So, after he
felt sure that peace and confidence had been restored in the
household, he began to weave the next step in his elaborate deception.

One night, with all of the fabricated sincerity he could
muster, Iktomi related to his wife the following wholly
untrue and outrageous story. Of course, he told her that it
was to be kept in the greatest of secrecy and she should be
honored to be privy to the plans of the Fox Society. He proceeded in a hushed voice, "My beloved, the Fox Society is
planning a prolonged and dangerous war campaign. So long
and dangerous will it be that only the strongest and the
bravest will be allowed to go. Now, as you probably do not
know, my sweet, it is the tradition of the Fox Society to call
the warriors for a campaign by acclamation. When they are
called, they step into the center of the circle until the
required number of warriors are chosen. I, your Iktomi,
was among the first chosen for this very dangerous, but
honorable, mission.

"When I reached the center, I told my brothers that I
was greatly honored. I told them that they had chosen
wisely, for I would most certainly be among the first to
confront the enemy. Nonetheless, I declined because the
society had actually decided to have each warrior take his

mother-in-law with him. Can you imagine that—actually thinking that each warrior's mother-in-law should accompany him to carry the supplies and provisions for the raid? That is just improper and downright wrong. I told them that I would have no part of it!"

Iktomi's wife might have been foolish, but she was not that foolish! She found his story so implausible, so outside of Lakota tradition, that she hardly comprehended all that he had said. *Oh no,* thought Iktomi, *she is becoming suspicious.* He told her the entire plan of the Fox Society again, giving special attention to the role of the mothers-in-law in their plan, but this did not help his cause. His wife was even more dumbfounded than before. She had never heard of such a thing!

The clever Iktomi thought that he had better be quiet for a while and let all that he had told his wife sink in. He believed that to push the matter any further at the moment might injure his cause. He had planted the seed, and he knew that his wife would in due time tell her mother and that the two women would talk the entire matter over. He was placing his hopes with his mother-in-law. The Fox Society was known for its nobility and courage, and this, coupled with the society's willingness to defend the tribe, would surely sway his wife's mother. She would not want to go against the wishes of such a worthy and respected society of warriors.

So Iktomi busied himself with tribal matters, allowing his plan to take hold while he appeared to be a responsible and mature member of the tribe. Just as he had hoped, his mother-in-law came to him and said that she was willing to honor the wishes of the Fox Society. After all, it was the least that she could do for such a selfless and noble group.

While her mother's decision greatly saddened Iktomi's wife, *he* was ecstatic. His nefarious and ignoble dream looked like it might actually come true. However, to keep his ruse above all suspicion, he continued to denounce the Fox Society's plans to have their mothers-in-law accompany them on such a dangerous mission. "I still say this is wrong," he passionately told the two women. "Women should not go on the warpath. It defies all tradition and common sense, not to mention all notions of right and wrong!

"I cannot understand it," Iktomi continued. "The Fox Society is above reproach—as worthy and noble a group as one could find. I am, indeed, so honored to a member of our elite warriors, but I just cannot make sense of all this."

The important thing now was to keep both women so busy that they would not have time to think about the matter or question others. He had them gather food to eat on the extended journey, clean and sharpen all his weapons, and make extra moccasins and robes. Iktomi pushed them day and night to get ready for the journey. He wanted to get on his way as soon as possible and, more important, he wanted to be sure to avoid having anyone ask any questions that might arouse suspicion.

When the women had most all of the preparations done, Iktomi supposedly hurried away to the Fox Society to get an update on the plans. He returned all excited and breathless, crying, "Hurry, hurry! Many of the warriors have already left, so we are going to have to catch up with them."

The women stood in disbelief, for warriors always left together in a party. Iktomi had to think quickly.

"Well, the Fox Society finally agreed with me," he explained. "They realized that taking their mothers-in-law with them in a war party certainly parted with tradition and could be seen as quite unseemly. Therefore, in order to avoid any questioning or criticism of their plan, they decided that each warrior should leave separately late at night and go in different directions. We will later all rendezvous at a prede-termined place. We had better get moving so that we are not left behind."

Iktomi was satisfied that he had explained away the incredulity of the two women. So, as darkness began to settle upon the village, Iktomi and his mother-in-law hastily gathered together all their provisions and weapons. Iktomi then gave a tearful and heartrending farewell to his young wife. Then, with great stealth, Iktomi and the older woman blended into the night and began their journey to war in distant lands.

After Iktomi and his mother-in-law had marched for several hours, he told her that they must be getting close to the rendezvous spot. Since it was very dark out and Iktomi could see very little, he cried out, "Where are you, my brothers?" He then cleverly put his robe over his mouth so as to disguise his voice and make it appear to be far away. By doing this, he was able to project a voice answering, "We are over here, brother!" His mother-in-law was so taken by this trick that Iktomi could not help himself from playing it a few more times as they journeyed forward. She was not the least bit suspicious, since she had complete trust in her son-in-law. After all, only the most courageous, most stead-fast, and most honorable young men were chosen for membership in the Fox Society. There was not a question in the woman's mind that soon they would be joining the other warriors and their mothers-in-law.

As they traveled on, Iktomi's calls always elicited the same response: "Over here!" It was getting late and Iktomi was getting tired of his ruse, so he decided that they had best stop for the night and camp. His weary mother-in-law agreed. Iktomi knew that he had best keep up the strict formality between in-laws, so he erected a hut made of grass. However, he let her know that it was for her alone— he would stand guard outside for the remainder of the night.

The exhausted mother-in-law quickly made her bed and peacefully settled in for the night, knowing that her son-in-law was on guard. The night was most comfortable for sleeping, and she was soon pleasantly and soundly slumber-ing. But a restful night it was not to be—no sooner had she begun to dream of roasting buffalo under a large cotton-wood tree then she was awakened by the sound of some-thing that sounded like a cross between a crying child and a whimpering dog. And she could hear the constant rattling of chattering teeth in the now-chilly night.

Of course it was Iktomi. "Oh, what shall I do?" he whined loud enough for her to hear. "I am freezing, and my robe does not seem to be able to keep the chill out."

His mother-in-law felt sorry for poor Iktomi. It was senseless for him to be so uncomfortable while she was so nicely nestled in the hut he had made. So she shouted, "Iktomi, please come in here—there is more than enough room for the two of us. There is no need for you to freeze to death!"

Iktomi was up in an instant and inside the hut. *Aha,* he thought, *another small victory! Soon I shall have my heart's desire!*

His mother-in-law settled comfortably back into bed, anxious to reenter the deep sleep that she had been in. Again, it was not to be—no sooner had she began to doze off then she heard Iktomi's whimpering and the chattering of his teeth. *He is still not warm,* she thought. *How can my warrior son-in-law ever be ready to meet the enemy without a good night's sleep? If he gets sick, he shall really be hampered in battle.* Realizing that she had to do what she could to warm up the freezing Iktomi, she said, "Come and lie down here, Iktomi."

Ah, these were the sweetest words Iktomi had ever heard! Before she could change her mind, he slipped under her buffalo robes next to her full, warm body.

Iktomi's ignoble and selfish plan was more easily unfolding than even he could have imagined! Away from all others, he was now lying next to the woman of his dreams. As he reviewed the many deceits it took him to get to the place of his desire, Iktomi was quite pleased with himself. *How clever I am!* he thought with great satisfaction.

Naturally Iktomi's chattering teeth came to a halt, and his "freezing" limbs were now warm and supple, but he was not satisfied with what to him was only a partial victory. Soon his lust-driven hands made slow but determined explorations of his mother-in-law's body. He focused on just her extremities at first, for he knew that he must be cautious so as not to forfeit the gains he had made so far. When it came to what he wanted, Iktomi was always both clever and careful.

The touch of his beloved's arm and then her knee sent wild passion throughout Iktomi, and her wonderful feminine odor only increased his ardor. As for his mother-in-law, it had been years since she had had a man next to her, much less caressing her. With the natural passion that all Lakota women carry deep within them, she began to feel an exciting warmth creep over her, and her receptivity to Iktomi begin to grow. Iktomi could feel this, and his own energies were fueled. Soon, all the sexual eagerness of her early youth broke forth in response to Iktomi's gently caressing hands and warm male body next to hers. All concern with propriety left with the smoke from the cozy hut, and they fulfilled their now-mutual passion.

However, in the light of day, guilt, remorse, and self-recrimination set in for the poor woman. She remained inside all day while Iktomi wandered about, supposedly looking for his not-to-be-found comrades. During his wanderings, Iktomi was filled with self-satisfaction at the complete success of his months of planning. Of course, his mother-in-law's feelings did not bother him in the least as he gloated over his conquest. He would find a way to overcome her guilt and remorse. If nothing else, Iktomi was always confident that his selfish plans would work out.

For the woman, though, things were very different. She felt great shame and could not even face her son-in-law. She fed Iktomi his meals without looking at him and refrained from conversation the entire day, which seemed to drag out forever as it does when our pain is great. Yet as the afternoon turned to evening and the star-filled sky began to appear, her remorse began to ebb. Now Iktomi's footsteps began to ignite warmth in her body, which had for so many years been denied pleasure. At the very touch of his hand, the terrible guilt and shame began to recede, as does the snow in the bright sunshine of spring. Her passion was again aroused.

After their second night together, they began to live as man and wife, and it was like a long, protracted honeymoon for them both. She was so happy to again feel like a woman and to be so appreciated, while he was ecstatic to have the understanding and the experience of a grown and mature woman. So they settled into an idyllic life. They would move their camp to one beautiful setting after another in the exquisite southern Black Hills. At times they camped deep in the canyons where they could bathe and swim by the moonlight, as if the whole world and all its magnificent beauty were theirs alone. At other times they could be found high in the hills, while the wind blew the fragrant scent of pine all around them. They lived as their hearts desired, and every night Iktomi fulfilled the ardent desire that had set all his plans into motion.

Life was good, and soon the couple had a large tipi. While Iktomi hunted among the more-than-plentiful game, his mother-in-law turned the rough hides of the animals into the softest of clothing and cured all the meat to provide for them on their travels. Before long, the tipi was filled with little ones. The woman loved nourishing and caring for her growing family, and what a large and robust family it had become!

Iktomi should have been proud and well satisfied, as was his mother-in-law. But as you have probably guessed, Iktomi could not remain satisfied for long with anything. He was a child who only pretended to be a man when it helped him achieve what he wanted. Consequently, he grew both dissatisfied and irritable. Why shouldn't he? He was Iktomi, destined to be a man of great standing, maybe even a chief! *This life of exile is not serving me,* he thought. *Furthermore, there is no one here to appreciate the great talents and abilities that I possess. I belong back with the People, where I can be honored as I should.*

When he expressed these thoughts to his mother-in-law, she remained silent, for she was wise enough to know that Iktomi was no extraordinary man at all and most ordinary at best. She had accepted that Iktomi would always be lost in his grand illusions and that what he could not accomplish by character and moral fiber he would do so by both deceit and manipulation. In fact, his daily delusional boasting and grandiosity were wearing her down. She was tired of hearing him talk about himself.

Iktomi decided that they should return to Lakota society, where he could take the respected position he was destined for. At the very thought of his future as a leader and respected tribal counselor, his spirits lifted as they began their march home.

Foolish dreamer! thought his mother-in-law. *He has no idea of the disdainful and shameful reception that we will receive upon arriving at the village. For all his brilliant conniving and deceit, poor Iktomi is a fool—a grandiose, self-indulgent fool!*

But nothing could shake Iktomi's dreams as he marched toward home with ever-greater dreams of grandiosity and narcissistic fulfillment. As the family approached the village, Iktomi's mother-in-law at last openly expressed her concern, which affected Iktomi not in the least.

"Do not worry, woman," he assured her. "I have outsmarted and outmaneuvered the wisest of men before, and I shall again. You will see! I, of course, have a plan already. I shall tell them how I, alone, with only the aid of my mother-in-law, have kept our enemies on the run and away from the People for all this time. They shall be so impressed with my courage and so appreciative of what I have done for one and all that they shall reinstate us into the village with the highest of honors! Just you wait and see."

That night the family camped out on a hilltop overlooking the village. Iktomi wanted to wait there until a scout saw them and would give them a welcoming sign. By doing so, he could have the scout return to the village before them and request a council meeting between himself and the elders upon his arrival. Thus, Iktomi sought to avoid any negative gossip before he could enact his plan and recount his noble deeds to the elders. He was sure that he would emerge a triumphant hero from the council tipi.

Before the council of elders, Iktomi related his tale of courage. With each masterful rendering of his bravery and steadfastness, he was sure that the elders were more than impressed. It had all started, he told them, with the blame-worthy Fox Society. He had trusted them, and in their trickery they had made what seemed to him a misguided plan, which flew in the face of all tradition and decorum. Nonetheless, both he and his mother-in-law had observed the strictest of protocol and were morally blameless. And as for the children, well, any warrior of honor and compassion would never harm a child or leave him alone and uncared for on a bloody battlefield. Of course, his only course of action was to take the children along with him and care for them as if they were his own. And this he had done.

"For, as you can see, the children are healthy and well cared for. Any mother and father would be proud of them," Iktomi said.

The elders sat in council, silent and unimpressed, hiding, for the moment, their contempt for this pitiful man and allowing Iktomi to weave his tale of lies into an increasingly incriminating web. Finally, they gave a signal, and Iktomi and his mother-in-law were briskly escorted outside, where a large group of warriors had formed a gauntlet. The warriors untied their breechclouts, which they used as short whips as Iktomi and his mother-in-law were made to the run the gauntlet. The swatting of the breechclouts themselves was not very painful, but that was not the intent of the gauntlet. It was the Lakota way of showing contempt—for those who ran the gauntlet, it was the most humiliating of experiences imaginable.

After they passed through the gauntlet, both Iktomi and his mother-in-law were banished from their village. There was no punishment greater than the banning of an individual from his tribe or village. The two miscreants were not allowed to keep the children they had brought into the world together; instead, they were adopted out to families in the village.

Thus, Iktomi's selfish scheming came to an end. But, as with all selfish behavior, he was not the only one injured— no, his wife, his mother-in-law, and his children also suffered as a result of his behavior.

CHAPTER TEN

Iktomi Cries "Wolf"

A s usual, Iktomi was out for a walk and looking for some mischief he could get into. However, this was an unusual day for him because he had been out for more than an hour and had yet to find a single person or animal to play a nasty trick on.

As he came out of the forest into the grassy flatlands, Iktomi spied a herd of elk. It had been a wonderful summer for grazing, for the fields had gotten a more-than-generous amount of rain. With such plush grass to eat, the elk were well fed and their coats were glossy. And thanks to the bounty of summer, their huge antlers rose toward the sky even more impressively than usual. One could not help but admire their grace, dignified bearing, and awesome power.

Needless to say, Iktomi envied these beautiful animals. He went to a nearby stream for a refreshing drink of water, and there he saw his reflection. "Oh, look at me compared to an elk!" Iktomi muttered to himself. "I am little, ugly, and of no real account in the world."

He went back toward the magnificent herd to look for the tallest and stateliest among them, and one clearly stood out from the rest. Iktomi was sure that he must be the chief, so he approached him (obsequiously, of course, for Iktomi was a master of manipulation).

"Good morning, uncle," Iktomi ventured. "You must be the chief. You look so strong and handsome; in fact, you are probably the most majestic elk chief I have ever met, and I, of course, have met many an elk chief. Look at me: My hair is not glossy; I am weak and small; and compared to you, oh mighty chief, I am nothing. However, there *is* one thing that we share. Everyone knows that elk are infused with love medicine—women just fall in love with you the moment they see you. It is real magic! But I am a truly wonderful lover as well."

"You must be pulling my leg," the chief said. "You do not look like much of a lover to me!"

Iktomi was unfazed by the chief's obvious disbelief. "My dear uncle," he replied, "you have the power to do most anything, so would you please make me a member of your tribe? I want so much to be just like you!"

"I don't know. . . . I have heard about you, Iktomi. You hold very little honor among your own people. Indeed, you have a terrible reputation. Why would I ever let you into my tribe?" asked the elk chief.

"All those things that you have heard about me are untrue! People are really jealous of me, and you know how jealous people behave when you have something that they don't," answered Iktomi.

"What could you possibly have to make people jealous of you?" replied the incredulous chief.

"Why, it is the same thing that you have, my good chief," Iktomi said. "I have tremendous luck with women—they just adore me."

"Well, I do not know if that is true, but many people *have* told me that you are a cry-baby coward," the chief retorted.

"Oh, buffalo dung," said Iktomi with feigned anger. "Again, they are just so jealous of me. I should wring their lying necks! The truth is, I am a powerful warrior with many scalps to my credit. I am untouchable, and I have the eagle feathers to prove it."

"Well, if that is true, then let me ask you some questions. How good are your eyes? Can you spot an enemy far in the distance like a good scout?" asked the chief, who was still not too sure about Iktomi.

"Chief, even the hawks envy my eyesight," Iktomi responded. "In fact, I bet that they were some of the ones who have slurred me to you."

"No, I have heard nothing from the hawk nation," said the chief. "But now, how about your hearing? Can you detect an enemy sneaking up to our camp to surprise us and cause us harm?"

"Come on, chief—no one has ears like mine! I can hear an ant from as far away as the stream that is about one hundred good elk strides from here," Iktomi answered.

"Well, all right, but how keen is your sense of smell, Iktomi? There are wolves, grizzly bears, and mountain lions all about, and they like nothing better than tasty elk meat. Can you sniff them out from afar? Can you track their scent to tell us the direction that they are traveling so that my tribe can avoid them?" the chief queried.

"Are you kidding me? I can detect a mouse's fart from here to Bear Butte," Iktomi bragged. "Do you know anyone else who can do that? I can even do it upwind!"

"In truth, I must say that I know of no one, not even the keenest dog, who can do that," admitted the amazed chief. "You know, you just might make a valuable member of my tribe."

"Oh, thank you, my noble chief! There is only one problem: I wouldn't want to be a member of your most worthy tribe, as small as I am. I mean, look at me—I am like a reed compared to a massive oak tree when I stand beside you. No one is going to believe all the wonderful talents I can bring to the tribe as long as I am this puny. Now, I have heard of your great power. They say that you can do almost anything you please, so why not make me as stately, handsome, and tall as yourself? Then I shall be able to perform my duties for the tribe with respect from all."

"Hmm, perhaps you are right," the chief answered. "Just stay right where you are, and I shall make you all those things that you asked for."

"Oh, one more thing, my chief. Could you please give me a pair of fearsome and powerful antlers?" Iktomi asked most humbly. "After all, what kind of an elk would I be without them?"

"You are right—who ever heard of a bull elk without antlers?" agreed the chief.

"But wait! Before you perform your magic on me, there is just one last thing I would like: a bountiful and glossy coat like yours, uncle. I must say that you are the most handsome elk that I have ever seen!" Iktomi proclaimed.

"Now, Iktomi, that is enough," the chief said. "Greed does not become an elk, especially an elk of my tribe. Anyway, here goes!" And he twirled his gigantic antlers three times to the west and then three times to the east.

Iktomi was instantly transformed into a bull elk every bit as imposing as the chief. In a heartbeat, Iktomi was dancing and prancing around as if he were the chief himself. He then proclaimed to his elk sisters and brothers, "Have you ever seen an elk as majestic as I? Have you ever seen an elk so strong and so powerful?"

Iktomi was, indeed, made a member of the chief elk's tribe, and he was accepted among his brothers and sisters with no trouble, for elks respect size and power, and, if the truth were known, they are terribly fond of good looks.

About a month later, the elk herd was all resting under the shade of some cottonwood trees when a small twig fell and struck Iktomi on the back.

"Run for your life!" screamed Iktomi. "I have been shot with an arrow! Run, run! There are hunters and ferocious grizzly bears about!"

Naturally, the herd sprang to its feet and was soon stampeding away as fast as it could. In front of them all was Iktomi, who was supposedly leading them away from great danger.

After running like the daylights for a mile or so, the herd realized that they were running from nothing. "There is nothing in sight, Iktomi," the herd said. "You were scared by nothing. Do not ever do that again—you frightened our little ones!"

The elk did not fully understand what a fearful little creature Iktomi was. A few days later, the herd was again resting in the shade, when an acorn fell and landed on Iktomi's back. Again, his screams alerted the herd: "Help, help! I have been hit by a bullet! Run as fast as you can, for there are hunters somewhere!"

The entire herd stampeded away, with Iktomi in the lead once more. And again the herd discovered that it was all alone on the vast prairie. "Iktomi, we have told you before never to send out a false alarm," the elk family scolded. "Getting the entire herd frightened and disturbed is serious business. We simply cannot have this if you are going to be a member of our tribe. You look like the grandest of elks, but you seem to have the heart of sparrow."

Of course, about a week or so later, the elk were contentedly grazing, when some thorns scratched Iktomi. "Ow!" he cried. "A hunter has stabbed me with a knife! An evil wolf is tearing at my flesh! Run, *run* for your lives!"

But this time, no one ran. In fact, no one even bothered to look up. Elk are very wise, and you are not going to fool them a third time, no matter how sincere you may appear to be.

The elk chief approached Iktomi and said, "Stop it right now, Iktomi. There are no wolves and there are no hunters. You have been told on two occasions to stop scaring everyone. You are both a liar and a coward. A mighty warrior, huh? Buffalo dung, I say—and a large pile of it, too!"

If you can believe it, this was not the end. Not two days later, the elk family heard Iktomi scream again: "Help! Help! Wake up and flee! The enemy is all about—there is a whole tribe of them!"

It was a bright, moonlit night, and the aroused elk could see a little baby rabbit hopping all around Iktomi. "Can you believe it?" the elk said to one another. "Iktomi was frightened out of his wits by a baby rabbit!" And they all began to laugh.

The next morning at sunrise, the elk could be seen whispering to one another. They were talking about Iktomi while he was down at the stream watering himself.

As night approached, the herd went to bed as usual. It was a good night for sleeping, and when Iktomi awoke well past sunrise, there was not an elk to be seen. He was all alone—and worse than that, he was no longer an elk. His beautiful, glossy coat was gone, as were as his antlers.

Iktomi stood alone, sorrowful little coward that he was. He had cried "hunter," "wolf," and "grizzly bear" for the last time.

Chasing Deer: Story time is over now, Grandson. Time for a little more buffalo stew and a good night's sleep! *Mitakuye Oyasin.*

Afterword

"These primitive people are habitually and universally the happiest
people I ever saw. They thoroughly enjoy the present, make no worry
over the possibilities of the future, and never cry over spilt milk. . . .
The Native American man never broods. . . . Among themselves,
the members of the family are perfectly easy and unrestrained.
It is extremely rare that there is quarreling among the wives.
There is no such thing as nervousness in either sex.
Everybody in the lodge seems to do just as he or she pleases,
and this seems no annoyance to anybody else."

— Col. Richard I. Dodge

"In our language, there is no word to say inferior or superior
or equality because we are all equal, it's a known fact.
But life has become complicated since the newcomers came here.
And how does your spirit react to it?
It's painful."

— Alanis Obomsawin, Abenaki

All of us, even the most pained and warped, want to be loved, to feel secure, to feel worthwhile, to feel ourselves as part of something larger and more important than just us. If Abraham Maslow is correct, then we cannot move on to higher ways of being until lower needs are satisfied. These lower needs are not just for food, oxygen, shelter, and so forth; they're also psychological and emotional. Only when these needs are satisfied can we be free to become ourselves, to truly love others, and to see beauty and values beyond mere physical existence. Only then can we become what Maslow called "self-actualized." A self-actualized person is self-directed, not other-directed—and as such, he is free to the extent that the society in which he lives allows him to be. (There are no nation-states upon this Earth in which a man is free—even our so-called freedom in the United States is only relative. Sure, there are more oppressive countries than ours, but do not mistake what we have in this country for freedom.)

In the movie *Thunderheart,* Val Kilmer plays Ray Levoi, an FBI agent sent to Pine Ridge Reservation (of the Oglala Lakota) to try to find and arrest an American Indian Movement (AIM) activist played by real-life AIM member John Trudell. Trudell's character, Jimmy Looks Twice, is being framed for a murder that was in reality the doing of the FBI itself. The story is a fictionalized account (for dramatic effect) of the kinds of things that were going on at Pine Ridge during the late '60s and much of the '70s. During this time, the FBI executed no less than 62 Indian activists, only one of whom was ever investigated, contrary to federal law.

Afterword

In any event, Ray Levoi begins to see things from the perspective of the Lakota as a result of his interactions with an ancient medicine man, and he becomes suspicious about what really happened. He goes to the old man's cabin and finds Jimmy Looks Twice with the old medicine man, and the following exchange occurs:

Ray: Get out of here. They will kill you.

Jimmy: They have to kill us because they cannot break our spirit.

Ray: What makes you such a threat?

Jimmy: We choose to be who we are. We know the difference between the reality of freedom and the illusion of freedom. There is a way to live with Earth and a way not to live with Earth. We choose the way of Earth.

I firmly feel that tribalism is the way of the Earth, and the only path to true social, political, and individual freedom. In fact, a theme running through this book has been that humans are by nature tribal animals. The farther we move away from this natural society, the more we disintegrate and become dysfunctional. For example, genocidal warfare was unknown to the American Indian, as was the slaughter of noncombatants, which the Pentagon inhumanly refers to as "collateral damage." There was only a slight difference between "rich" and "poor"; while theft, bribery, rape, lying, and mental illness were all virtually unknown. There were no homeless, there were no hungry, and there were no disenfranchised. Indeed, if you were to take all the many ills that now plague our modern world, you would find few of them in tribal culture. Such problems are the result of "civilization" and its propensity for placing more value on property than on the quality of human life . . . or life itself.

I find it rather telling that the United States and the countries of Western Europe are considered first-world countries, while tribal people are considered to be part of the third world. Obviously, this distinction is based upon two things: economics and technology. Were the distinctions based on justice, fairness, honesty, spirituality, and the like, the situation would be reversed: We would be classified as a third-world society, while tribal people would belong to the first world.

As I said in the Introduction, one of the great differences between many Indian cultures and those of the Western world is that, for the most part, Indians took the wisdom and the teachings of its cultural heroes and spiritual leaders very seriously. This is well shown in the Lakota name of Jason James, my medicine man's assistant: Walks with His Word. The Western Euro-American world does not and has not. As a result, the American Indian lived a far more satisfying life than we are even capable of imagining.

As George Sauer, a leading authority on the first contact between Europeans and American Indians wrote:

Afterword

The tropical idyll of the account of Columbus and Peter Martyr was largely true. The people suffered no want. They took care of their plantings, were dexterous in fishing, and bold canoeists and swimmers. They designed attractive houses and kept them clean. They found aesthetic expression in woodworking. They had leisure to enjoy diversions in ballgames, dances, and music. They lived in peace and amity.

While the above was written about the Caribbean Indians the Europeans first encountered, the same could have been written about many tribes on the American continents (disregarding, of course, the geographical and climatic references).

Let me share with you a few of the many first written accounts of what the Europeans found when they first came across Indians. In his *Journals,* Columbus noted:

> And the people are so gentle.... The houses of these Indians are the most beautiful I have ever seen.... They are well swept and quite clean inside, and the furnishings are arranged in good order ... these are [the] friendliest people.... There cannot be better or more gentle people than these anywhere in the world ... the Chiefs are men of few words and fine manners, it is a marvel.... [T]hey are so artless and free with all they possess, that no one would believe it without having seen it. Of anything that they have, if you ask them for it, they never say no; rather, they invite the person to share it, and show as much love as if they were giving their hearts; and whether the thing

be of value or small price, at once they are content with whatever little thing of whatever kind may be given to them.

Amerigo Vespucci penned:

> ... a race I say [is] gentle and amenable. ... They live together without king, without government, each is his own master. They live one hundred and fifty years, and rarely fell ill, and if they do fall victim to any disease, they cure themselves with certain roots and herbs.

A captain of Pizarro, Mancio Serra de Lehuezana, dictated the following on his deathbed:

> That we discovered these riches in such condition that there was not in all of them one thief, one vicious man, nor was there an adulterous woman or bad woman ...

Finally, Arthur Barlowe, one of the first Englishmen to land in Virginia, wrote:

> ... we were entertained with all love and kindness and with as much bounty, after their manner, as they could possibly devise. We found the people most gentle, loving, and faithfull, void of all guile and treason, and such as lived after the manner of the Golden Age ... a more kind and loving people, there cannot be found in the world, as Farre as we have hitherto had triall.

Were these a happy people? Two writers who lived with the Plains Indians wrote:

> The common belief that the Indian is stoical, stolid, and sullen is altogether erroneous. They are really a merry people, good-natured and jocular, usually ready to laugh at an amusing incident or joke, with a simple mirth that reminds one of children.... I don't believe I ever heard a real hearty laugh away from the Indian's fireside. I have often spent an entire evening with them, until I could laugh no more.

As long ago as the late 16th century, Sir Francis Bacon said:

> It has often been seen that a Christian gentleman, well-borne and bred, and gently nurtured, will, of his own free will, quit his high station and luxurious world, to dwell with savages and live their lives, partaking in all their savagery. But never yet hath it been seen that a savage will, of his own free will, give up his savagery and live the life of a civilized man.

(It should be noted that "savage" here and in the following does not carry the same meaning as the word today. In essence, it referred to people who lived in a state of nature as opposed to "civilization.")

In his classic *The History of the Five Nations of Canada,* which was published in 1727, Cadwallader Colden wrote:

No Arguments, no Intreaties, nor Tears of their Friends and Relations, could persuade many of them to leave their new *Indian* Friends and Acquaintance[s], several of them that were by the Caressings of their Relations persuaded to come Home, in a little Time grew tired of our Manner of living, and run away again to the *Indians,* and ended their Days with them. On the other hand, *Indian* Children have been carefully educated among the *English,* cloathed and taught, yet, I think, there is not one Instance, that any of these, after they had Liberty to go among their own People, and were come to Age, would remain with the *English,* but returned to their own Nations, and became as fond of the *Indian* Manner of Life as those that knew nothing of a civilized Manner of living.

On May 9, 1753, Benjamin Franklin wrote to Peter Collinson:

> When an Indian Child has been brought up among us, taught our language and habituated to our Customs . . . yet if he goes to see his relations and make one Indian Ramble with them, there is no perswading him ever to return. [But] when white persons of either sex have been taken prisoners young by the Indians, and lived a while among them, tho' ransomed by their Friends, and treated with all imaginable tenderness to prevail with them to stay among the English, in a Short time they become disgusted with our manner of life, and the care and pains that are necessary to support it, and take the first Opportunity of escaping again into the Woods, from whence there is no reclaiming them.

Afterword

What the previous three writers wrote did not refer to just a few, but rather thousands of white people from all stations of life who chose to "become Indians." Simply put, they found in Indian life the same values that, in many instances, their own culture voiced but did not live and could not live because of the very structure of the society itself.

The ethnohistorian James Axtell sums up very well why some many Euro-Americans "became Indians." He writes:

> The great majority of white Indians left no explanation for their choice. Forgetting their original language and their past, they simply disappeared into their adopted society. But those captives who returned to write narratives of their experiences left several clues to the motives of those who chose to stay behind. They stayed because they found Indian life to possess a strong sense of community, abundant love, and uncommon integrity—values that the English colonists also honored, if less successfully. But Indian life was attractive for other values—for social equality, mobility, adventure, and, as two adult converts acknowledged, "the most perfect freedom, the ease of living, [and] the absence of those cares and corroding solicitudes which so often prevail with us." As we have learned recently, these were values that were not being realized in the older, increasingly crowded, fragmented, and contentious communities of the Atlantic seaboard, or even in the newer frontier settlements. By contrast, as Crevecoeur said, there must have been in the Indians' "social bond something singularly captivating." Whatever it was, its power had no better measure than the

large number of English colonists who became, contrary to the civilized assumptions of their countrymen, white Indians.

It would be arrogant to say that the teachings of Dekanahwideh, Sweet Medicine, and White Buffalo Calf Maiden were superior to those of Jesus or Buddha or even much of Thomas Jefferson. The only difference is that in the egalitarianism of tribal life and in the meeting of the basic needs of *all* the people, the teachings of these great cultural heroes found the soil in which they could both grow and flourish.

I can only hope that humanity recognizes that the deadly detour it has taken from our natural social organization will eventually lead to our extinction. Unfortunately, I am not holding my breath. So, I pray and go the sweat lodge.

Acknowledgments

I would like to thank the following people: Reid Tracy, for asking me to write another book for Hay House; Jill Kramer and Shannon Littrell, without whose editorial guidance this book may never have been completed; and finally, to Lucy Bacon, for her help in making some of these stories more accessible to the contemporary reader.

About the Author

Kurt Kaltreider, Ph.D., is of Nanticoke, German, and English descent. He graduated from Gettysburg College and holds an M.A. and Ph.D. in philosophy and clinical psychology from the University of Tennessee. Due to the erosion of traditional Indian cultures, Kurt devotes himself full time to the protection and support of the ways of his ancestors. He is the author of *American Indian Prophecies.*

Notes

Notes

Notes

Notes

Notes

Notes

Notes

We hope you enjoyed this Hay House book.
If you would like to receive a free catalog featuring additional
Hay House books and products, or if you would like information
about the Hay Foundation, please contact:

Hay House, Inc.
P.O. Box 5100
Carlsbad, CA 92018-5100

(760) 431-7695 or **(800) 654-5126**
(760) 431-6948 (fax) or **(800) 650-5115 (fax)**
www.hayhouse.com

Published and distributed in Australia by:
Hay House Australia, Ltd. • 18/36 Ralph St. • Alexandria NSW 2015
Phone: 612-9669-4299 • *Fax:* 612-9669-4144
www.hayhouse.com.au

Published and distributed in the United Kingdom by:
Hay House UK, Ltd. • Unit 62, Canalot Studios
222 Kensal Rd., London W10 5BN • *Phone:* 44-20-8962-1230
Fax: 44-020-8962-1239 • www.hayhouse.co.uk

Published and distributed in the Republic of South Africa by:
Hay House SA (Pty), Ltd., P.O. Box 990, Witkoppen 2068
Phone/Fax: 2711-7012233 • orders@psdprom.co.za

Distributed in Canada by:
Raincoast • 9050 Shaughnessy St., Vancouver, B.C. V6P 6E5
Phone: (604) 323-7100 • *Fax:* (604) 323-2600

Sign up via the Hay House USA Website to receive the Hay House
online newsletter and stay informed about what's going on with your
favorite authors. You'll receive bimonthly announcements about:
Discounts and Offers, Special Events, Product Highlights,
Free Excerpts, Giveaways, and more!
www.hayhouse.com